THE
MACMILLAN
BOOK
OF ORGANIC GARDENING

MARIE-LUISE KREUTER

THE MACMILLAN BOOK

OF ORGANIC GARDENING

Translated by Susan H. Ray

COLLIER BOOKS
MACMILLAN PUBLISHING COMPANY
NEW YORK

COLLIER MACMILLAN PUBLISHERS
LONDON

Contents

Macmillan Publishing Company
866 Third Avenue, New York, N.Y. 10022
Collier Macmillan Canada, Inc.

Title of the original German edition:
1 X 1 des Bio-Gärtnerns
© 1983 BLV Verlagsgesellschaft mbH,
München

English translation copyright © 1985 by
Macmillan Publishing Company, a division of Macmillan, Inc.

Library of Congress Cataloging in
Publication Data

Kreuter, Marie-Luise.
    The Macmillan book of organic gar-
dening.
    Translation of: 1 x 1 des Bio-Gärt-
nerns.
    Includes index.
    1. Organic gardening.   I. Title.
SB453.5.K7413   1985   635′.0484
85-7274

ISBN 0-02-063150-2

10 9 8 7 6 5 4 3 2 1

Printed in Germany

Contents

Introduction

More and more people are turning to organic gardening. Many factors have led them to this decision: the ubiquitous pollution and wanton destruction of the environment, frequent reports about alarming crop failures, and fruits and vegetables from the supermarket that "taste like nothing."

In addition, increasing numbers of people are beginning to fear for their health and for the future of their children. They realize that we may not simply continue to plunder the earth with impunity. This is why many gardeners are once again trying to work with nature, not against it. At least one's own garden might once again offer a relaxed oasis where humans as well as animals and plants can live in as healthy and as natural a manner as possible.

Until recently, the majority of "traditional" home gardeners used to smile down upon the "organics" with a superior and haughty mien, calling them "green sectarians" and "kohlrabi apostles." Meanwhile, word has gotten out that the natural methods of gardening are really not some sort of madness. The photographs in this book, taken for the most part in the author's own garden, bear witness to the impressive results. Innumerable other organic gardeners can also attest to similar success with fertile soils and abundant harvests. Most importantly, however, they demonstrate that it is possible to maintain a healthy environment, at least within the bounds of one's own property.

The harvest from a carefully tended organic garden is impressive. The potatoes being dug up are healthy; their number and size are typical, but their particular advantage is that organically grown potatoes keep well and can be stored easily.

As more "traditional" gardeners become eager to realize the dream of a natural garden, there are ever greater demands for books that provide general and easy directions as to how to do this. After all, anyone who wants to become an organic gardener must first of all know how it is done. He or she needs only some initial success to become completely convinced and to stick with it.

Anyone can start an organic garden; there is no secret in the method. On the contrary, it is practical, natural, and easy to understand. One important precondition, however, is that the gardener be prepared to learn a little about the workings of nature by carefully observing the habits and life cycles of plants and animals.

This book is intended for just this purpose. It is meant primarily for the "greenhorn." You will find a brief introduction to the basics of the natural or organic method of gardening, but more importantly, perhaps, you will also discover some practical hints and suggestions concerning the most important tasks in your organic garden: the construction of a compost heap, the advantage of mulching and fertilizing with organic materials, information about mixed plantings and organic pest control. Included also are many tips for the organic raising of vegetables, fruits, and flowers.

Step boldly into the world of organic gardening! You will soon see a healthy and productive garden come to life under your very hands. I hope that this basic guide will ease you through the beginning stages, so that you will soon be successfully and happily gardening in tune with nature. The path from a hesitant beginner to an experienced old hand is not very long.

Why Organic Gardening?

Actually, a better question is, why not? Anyone who works consistently in keeping with organic methods can count on healthy plants, colorful flowers, and rich harvests. What more could a gardener want?

Why should you risk spraying with toxic insecticides when the job can be done with other means? The danger, of course, does not rest in the single application of an isolated preparation, but rather in the accumulation of many injurious substances that collect in the soil, in the water, and finally in the plants themselves.

No one knows precisely what insidious brew has been and continues to be absorbed over the years. We are nearly powerless against the environmental pollution caused by industry, agriculture, and automobiles. But in our own garden we can try to act in a healthier, a more natural, and thus a more responsible manner. Why should we spend a great deal of money every year for chemical insecticides, synthetic manures, and peat when there are other ways of accomplishing the same purpose? The organic method is more economical and more effective in the long run. The laws of nature are very economical: Compost and a liquid manure brewed from stinging nettles incur almost no expense, but they increase the productivity of the garden enormously.

Of course, there are times when, even in organic gardens, it will be necessary to spray. Organic gardeners, unlike traditional gardeners, use natural substances, the majority of which grow freely at the side of the road or along the garden fence. Such homemade sprays keep the plants healthy without endangering the environment.

Commercially produced organic products that can be very useful for fertilizing or for controlling pests are readily available. But the longer and the more closely a gardener works with nature, the less "outside help" will be needed. The results will be increased stability and fertility of the soil as well as healthier plants.

In recent years, many people have discovered, or are at least beginning to be aware, that there is something to this organic or natural method of gardening. But when asked why they want to start an organic garden, they usually give a negative reason: "I don't want to use poisons or commercial fertilizers!" Moreover, many gardeners, primarily the younger ones, also believe that in an organic garden everything should grow the way "Mother Nature" intended it to grow —without any fertilizers, without ever harming a single leg of a single louse. This is the rapid road to Green Chaos.

I have much more positive motivation. A genuine organic gardener is not a gardener at all, but an advocate. He or she is *for* the natural improvement of the soil, *for* compost and organic fertilizers, *for* gentle, natural means of pest control, *for* healthy fruit and vegetables. An organic gardener does not fight with belligerent weapons—neither against lice nor against gardeners of a different persuasion. A good example is more convincing in the long run than a torrent of harsh words. If, by stealing a glance over the garden fence, your neighbors see that you are reaping unblemished apples and plump tomatoes even without chemicals, then they may eventually think that, if it *is* possible, why

Pickles in a stoneware crock, prepared the way Grandmother used to do it, homemade marmalade, herbed vinegar and oils all preserve the healthy pleasures of the summer long into the winter months.

shouldn't they, too, try the organic route. And with this decision the number of those who take pains to create the most natural conditions possible within a small garden plot has grown by another convert or two.

Fruit and vegetables raised in gardens such as these can once again be considered nutritious food. No one need fear invisible deficiencies. Children can safely bite into freshly picked fruit, for, like their grownup counterparts, they, too, enjoy the refreshing taste of tomatoes and the sweet crunch of carrots. And it pays to put this home-grown harvest up for the winter. Such preserves are invaluable, because they are rich not only in natural aroma but in vitamins and minerals as well. And organically grown fruits are characterized by their resistance to spoilage.

Most important, however, is the fact that, after the toils of the summer,

organic gardeners know exactly what is in their fruit and what is definitely not in it. For this and many other reasons, it is a worthwhile endeavor to garden organically. The best way is to try it yourself, because personal experience is much more convincing than the power of persuasion.

These unblemished apples were never sprayed with insecticide.

What the Earth Is Made of

The basic material with which all gardeners work their whole life long is the earth. This brown, crumbly material is constantly changing. Earth is a living and thus unpredictable commodity. Only through understanding and care can it be made to produce the desired results. Whoever irresponsibly plunders the soil will sooner or later find himself a beggar. The rapidly expanding deserts all over the world ought to serve as a warning to us all.

Sandy soil flows through your fingers.

Soil and Its Characteristics

The soil is the basic dowry of any garden. Gardeners must respond to this dowry, which was included in their purchase of a house or a piece of property right from the start, and this means that they will have to deal with the individual characteristics of their native soil. It may consist of any one or even a combination of the following types:

Sandy Soil

These soils are light and porous. They consist of innumerable grains of sand that allow rainwater to filter as if through a sieve. Sandy soils retain neither moisture nor nutrients. They warm up quickly, but cool off just as quickly.

Nevertheless, sandy soils do have one advantage: They can be easily worked. A potato harvest, for example, requires much less work in a light soil such as this than in a heavier soil containing clay. But plants soon come to suffer from hunger and thirst in sandy soils. This is why organic gardeners have to enrich the light, grainy

earth with humus and "compacting" substances. Compost, peat moss, and mulches are very good for this purpose. Furthermore, pure sand is a rare commodity; the light, quartz-containing soil is usually combined with greater or lesser proportions of clay.

Loamy Soil

Here the gardener is fortunate, for he is standing on land rich in humus.

Loamy soil rich in humus is friable.

What the Earth is Made of

Loamy soils usually also contain lime. They are capable of storing water, nutrients, and warmth, all of which are necessary prerequisites for healthy plant life.

Loamy soils contain a varying amount of sand. Depending upon the mixture, they are either loose and humous or dense and heavy. All the procedures and suggestions for organic cultivation described in this book apply for the care of loamy soil. Most important is the routine addition of compost and mulches.

Clay Soil

This is the negative intensification of the loamy soil, for its structure is heavy and dense. Clay soils are cold and nonporous. It is very difficult for the roots of plants to penetrate this tough mass. When it rains, the water collects in puddles; during dry spells the ground becomes as hard as roof tiles.

Clay soils are basically fertile because they tend to retain nutrients, but they have to be improved consid-

You can make solid clumps of clay.

erably in their structure. This is frequently a painstaking task. In extreme cases sand must be added as a loosening agent, followed by a green manure that develops deep roots, which then produce the first airy pockets. With time, compost and mulch covers build up a surface layer rich in humus, and it is in this layer that the plants can thrive.

Marshy Soil

Highland marshy soils are moist and acidic and rich in peat, but by nature they are poor in nutrients. This is why the gardener has to help them along with the addition of stone meals that contain clay, along with compost, lime, and organic fertilizers.

Low marshy soils, on the other hand, do have a certain lime content; they are also less acidic than the highland varieties.

As a beginning gardener, you should take a handful of earth and get acquainted with it. Sand will flow through your fingers. Humus-containing loam can be compressed to a certain extent, but it remains crumbly and does not stick together. Clay forms tough clumps; you can make pottery out of it. Finally, marshy soil can be squeezed like a damp sponge.

Now you know what your garden has to offer. What you do with it during the next few years is your business as an organic gardener.

Living Humus

Dark brown, fragrant humus—that is the goal of every gardener who follows the rules of nature. Such a dream soil is loose, warm, moist, and rich in

What the Earth is Made of

nutrients. Vegetables, fruits, and flowers thrive in it almost without outside help.

Natural mixed forests are forever teaching us how humus comes into being. Whoever wants to get his hands on the fundamentals of organic gardening need only turn to nature for his lessons. Push aside the loose covering of leaves beneath the trees and use both hands to turn over the soil a few times. This experiment is not strenuous, for your hands will sink effortlessly into soft, gloriously dark earth. If you then close your eyes and inhale the scent of the forest ground, which smells a bit like mushrooms, you will know how the soil in your own garden should feel.

The forest accomplishes this miracle without spade or fertilizer sack. No human being interferes to nourish the trees and shrubs. And yet they grow to mighty proportions and frequently live much longer than the individuals who planted them.

The forest lives off its own waste. Every autumn, wilted leaves and

A natural leaf cover on the humus soil of the forest.

needles form a loose ground cover. Dried grasses, slender twigs, and animal waste all mix together. For microorganisms and small rodents, this is a groaning board, and they continuously transform the decomposing organic substances into nutrient-rich humus. In this way the good earth silently replenishes itself.

If someone were to decide to sweep the forests clean in the fall, this miraculous recycling procedure would collapse. The trees would no longer be able to feed themselves; the water table would be seriously disturbed. Without external, artificial nourishment, the forests would eventually die.

Even in your own garden, nature can provide, to a large extent, its own nourishment and precious humus. All you have to do is let it! "Mother Earth" is not a finished product, but a living organism. It is constantly changing, for better or for worse, in keeping with the way the gardener directs the life processes in his or her garden.

The Microcosm Under Our Feet

Every day we trample upon the greatest of miracles and the most patient of workers. Garden soil resembles a city organized down to the smallest detail, a city in which millions of inhabitants are at work day and night. A brief peek into this underground world will rapidly acquaint beginning organic gardeners with the most important laws of a natural garden.

The humus cover in the beds is divided into well-ordered layers. Although it is teeming with life, nothing happens accidentally. Most of the inhabitants of this microcosm in the earth are so indescribably tiny that they can be seen only with an electron

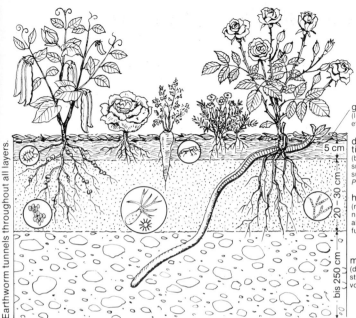

Earthworm tunnels throughout all layers.

ground cover
(leaves. grass,
etc.)

decomposi-
tion layer
(bacteria, fungus,
small animals
such as the
Poduridae)

5 cm

humus layer
(microorganisms,
nitrogen bacteria,
algae, vine-root
fungus)

20 – 30 cm

mineral layer
(disintegrated
stone, water reser-
voir)

bis 250 cm

A cross-section view of the ingenious organization of the soil layers.

microscope. They include microorganisms such as bacteria and algae, or
primitive forms of life like Flagellata
and Ciliata.

Small, visible animals also inhabit
our fertile Mother Earth, including
threadworms, springtails, millipedes,
centipedes, slugs and snails, and,
above all, earthworms. When left
undisturbed, they all work hand in
hand on the transformation of organic
waste into humus and various
nutrients.

This vital teamwork takes place in
three well-organized zones. The
uppermost layer in an organic garden
consists of a mulch cover. Under this
lies the first layer of humus, the so-
called decomposition zone. It is about
2″ deep. This is the home of the specialized microorganisms that start the

decomposition process. Wilted leaves,
blades of grass, small twigs, and even
dead bugs are taken apart here and
reduced in size. The creatures in this
later need oxygen, moisture, and
warmth for their work. Beneath their
feet begins the actual humus layer,
which can be as deep as 4″ to 12″.
Here completely different types of
microorganisms are at work. They
construct new building blocks of life
from the ingredients of the decomposition layer. Here, for example, is
where nutritive solutions which possess just the right composition for the
root systems of plants are engen-
dered. A close, reciprocal activity is
constantly taking place between the
organisms in the earth and the roots
of the plants.

The fertile, crumbly structure of

What the Earth is Made of

durable humus is also created in this second layer. It is composed of innumerable algae and fungi, all of which have definite tasks of their own to perform.

One of the most important concerns of organic gardeners is to protect and to care for these living layers. They should never be disturbed unnecessarily, because that destroys the network of closely knit relationships to the detriment of the soil, the plants, and the gardener. The natural care of humus is thus one of the most basic tasks of the organic gardener. Just how this knowledge is put to use in the garden can be learned from the chapter entitled "Spadework? No Thanks!"

The Cycle of the Elements

The living and nutrient-rich humus layer is normally 7" to 12" deep. Only small surfaces of the globe are covered by this most precious of all natural materials. All of us—human beings, animals, and plants—live on the products that this thin layer of Mother Earth generates. If this fertile soil should be lost, we would have no chance of survival.

Organic gardeners consciously and empathetically tend the soil temporarily assigned to their care. In doing so, they let billions of invisible assistants work for them. All organic garden waste, regardless of the season, can be returned to the soil, for it serves as nourishment for the organisms that convert this waste into new soil for our old earth. Thus the natural cycle of the elements has come full circle, and man, too, has once again assumed his rightful role in it.

This compost silo demonstrates the circulation of materials. Organic refuse is poured in from above and the new soil that forms from garden waste is removed from below.

Useless? Not in the Eyes of Nature

Only human beings could divide the rest of the world into categories of "good" and "bad," "useful" and "useless." This valuation is completely dependent upon the viewpoint of a creature that considers itself the ruler over all others. "Useful" for humans is whatever multiplies their selection of foodstuffs and whatever increases their material wealth. "Useless" are all those who dare to gnaw away at the products of human diligence.

There Is Actually No Such Thing as a "Garden Pest"

Ever since its very beginnings, the garden has always been a cultivated oasis carefully marked off from the "wilderness." Behind the protection of fences and hedges thrive cultivated plants that are larger and more productive than their untamed predecessors. These cultivated specimens, however, are simultaneously more sensitive to disease and more demanding as far as nourishment and outside care are concerned.

Traditional gardeners who go to a great deal of trouble to harvest thick bunches of celery and pails of sweet peas do not want to share these nutritious possessions with unwelcome guests. They therefore look upon every animal that turns up uninvited at their garden table as a "pest."

Every gardener has the right to protect his plants. After all, the object is to grow nutritious fruits and vegetables for the family. It is a shortsighted gardener, however, who kills every animal in his path simply because of this. The balance of nature is seriously disturbed by such harsh interference.

Organic gardeners must come to the sometimes uncomfortable realization that every "pest" is at the same time a welcome "guest." Lice, for example, provide food for ladybugs, titmice, and lacewing larvae. The total elimination of crawling or sucking insects also means the elimination of the necessary life conditions of numerous "guests." Even voracious slugs perform a positive task in the garden on the side, as it were: They do away with rotting waste and small, dead animals. This type of "garbage disposal" is important for many, and not just hygienic, reasons.

Although the garden is a cherished and, to a certain extent, artificial bit of the environment, what counts as the highest law here, too, is the harmony of all living creatures. The more successful the gardener is in establishing and maintaining the natural balance and reciprocal relations among them, the less he will have to interfere. Weak or overly fertilized plants are particu-

The caterpillars of the cabbage butterfly on a kohlrabi plant.

Useless? Not in the Eyes of Nature

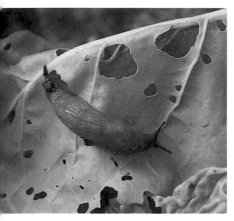

A brown slug on a tender beet leaf.

larly susceptible to pests. Lice prefer tender, weak tissue; they tend to avoid crisp, sturdy leaves. This is why the cultivation of healthy, strong plants is one of the preventive measures

organic gardeners can use to combat pests successfully. If the soil is healthy and tended with compost and mulch covers, the plants it supports will also be strong and resistant.

Raising a number of different fruits and vegetables helps guard against an unwieldy infestation and multiplication of those animals that rank as "pests" only when present in large numbers. A variety of different plants makes it difficult for them to spread out. If the fruit or vegetable changes with each row, insects or bugs that feed on special plants will have to find another home. Your neighbor, however, is often displeased with carefully planned mixed gardens, for many pests wander onto his property in their search for greener pastures.

An alternating variety of crops is easy to accomplish in the garden. It also satisfies the gardener's desire to

In this rural organic garden, vegetables, fruit, flowers, and herbs make a healthy combination.

Useless? Not in the Eyes of Nature

grow as many different varieties of fruits and vegetables as possible. Through careful planning, both the protection of the plants and an abundant yield are easily combinable goals.

The Function of Weeds

There are just as few "weeds" as there are "pests." Every wild plant that grows in the garden or along the path fulfills a specific purpose in the larger community of living creatures. Very frequently the undesirable plant a gardener impatiently pulls out turns out to be a medicinal herb containing valuable properties that can help maintain a person's health. But few people have the most rudimentary knowledge of such things anymore.

Organic gardeners, though, can learn even from "weeds," which can provide valuable tips concerning the condition of the soil, for no wild plant grows in a particular place by accident. The earth is rich in "sleeping" seeds, and these sprout only when they find the specific conditions that correspond to their personal taste.

Heavy, nonporous soils support a completely different group of plants than does a looser, humus soil. Anyone who takes the trouble to learn to recognize weeds and to understand their language will be rewarded with valuable ideas for his or her own garden work. Indicative of heavy, clumpy soil, for example, are dandelions, cornmint, and creeping cocksfoot. In damp subsoils one finds dockweed

Weeds can be a source of useful information for the gardener. Knotgrass *(Polygonum)* (above) indicates heavy, wet soil. Galinsoga (middle) grows in good humus. Spurge *(Euphorbia)* (below) thrives in alkaline soil.

17

Such pleasantly haphazard patches of wild flowers along the edges of fields are becoming increasingly rare nowadays.

and comfrey. Pansies and camomile indicate a paucity of lime. A good lime content, on the other hand, is signified by marigolds, meadow sage, germander, and caper spurge. If what meets the gardener's eye are chickweed, stinging nettles, deadly nightshade, and orach, there is no room for complaints. These weeds betray a good soil rich in humus.

Wild plants, however, do more than provide clear indications as to the condition of the earth in which they are growing; they also contribute to its transformation. Their roots help loosen the soil, and many plants, like clover, for example, even deposit nutrients in the soil. Others contribute to the regeneration of exhausted soils via root secretions. This is why in centuries past fields were left fallow for

one full year following three consecutive harvests. During this time wild flowers and weeds reclaimed the land. It recuperated and compensated for many deficiencies. Thus, "weeds" are medicine for the earth as well as for mankind. Unwelcome plants can often give the organic gardener good advice.

The desire for a plot of land where one can live with one's family without worrying about invisible noisome substances is common to most of us. But many people have not yet managed to turn their dream into green reality because they fear that the organic method involves too much effort or is too esoteric for traditional gardeners.

From a Dream to Green Reality

There is no such thing as *the* organic method. Rather than just one, there are several paths that lead naturally to a healthy garden. Many a narrow path is really meant for the specialist alone, but the middle path is broad and within the reach of everyone.

The main purpose of this book is to describe the procedures that underlie the biological-organic method. They can be applied anywhere at any time in any type of garden. I think it is extremely important that as many people as possible should once again be able to live in as natural and as healthy a garden as possible. This book, therefore, concentrates on those ideas and suggestions that are easily understood and, above all, practical. If at some future time the more advanced organic gardener decides to concentrate on specialized approaches, such as the organic-dynamic method, he or she can find a great deal of additional literature on this specific topic.

Patience in the Transition Period

Once a gardener has decided to switch over to the organic method, the first tools he or she will need are patience and perseverance. Nothing is more difficult than changing one's own habits. This is why it is essential that organic gardeners be patient with themselves. Even rethinking takes time! And the same holds true for the garden; it does not change from one minute to the next. After years of toxic chemical sprays and synthetic, com-

mercially produced salts and fertilizers, nature itself needs a little time to get back into the swing of things.

The diversity of life in the soil has to be carefully reestablished. A sufficient amount of space and the proper conditions have to be provided for the many guests the organic gardener will want to attract and foster.

Depending upon the particular conditions already existing in the garden, the transition period can bring some unpleasant surprises. Organic methods start to work well only after the ecological net has been respun by innumerable organisms. As long as any holes remain, pests and diseases can always slip in. Lice infestations, for instance, can be expected during

Compost is the foundation of an organic garden.

From a Dream to Green Reality

the transition period. Chemical means of pest control are gone, but the natural allies are not yet strong enough to maintain a balance. In extreme cases, organic sprays can help, and these are described in the chapter on "Pest Control."

The most important thing to remember, however, is this: Hold your ground! The future organic gardener is charged with the responsibility of performing, with care and regularity, each important step that lays the natural foundation of a garden. Adding compost and mulch covers is a constant job that cannot be neglected, for it is the only way to conquer dry soil. If you give up at this stage and reach for the insecticide, you will destroy more nutrients than you could ever lose through sheer neglect. You might find a temporary respite from the lice, but this is the peace of the cemetery.

The Biological Balance

Every garden reacts a little differently, but be assured that at some time—after two or three years, perhaps—the day will come when the organic gardener sees, feels, and knows that it's working! The biological balance will be visible everywhere: a harmonious coexistence between soil, plants, and animals. At this point the garden will finally be living according to the laws of nature. Life and death, health and disease will have attained a balance.

No man and no garden is ever perfect, but at least there will be no catastrophes in a balanced organic garden. The gardener will now be able to cope, without anxiety and without force, with the usual vicissitudes of life and weather.

And as new organic gardeners actually see how well their gardens are flourishing, when the gardens can develop naturally in the full sense of the word, they will no longer need to be convinced with words. They will have seen and felt with their own senses that this is right and this is good.

From a Dream to Green Reality

It Pays Off

An organic garden is a place of peace. Vegetables, fruits, and herbs can be harvested with no fear of toxic contamination. Children can eat fresh strawberries or apples right from the shrub or tree. The harvest is nutritious, tasty, and easily put up for later use. Fruits can once again fulfill their natural functions by providing both nourishment and healing. This means a great deal in an environment that is becoming increasingly unhealthy.

But the inner values are just as important as the tangible results. How can an individual find peace and relaxation if he has to fight roses and rhubarb for a place to sit down? In a natural garden he can be cheerful and calm. He is on the side of the life he is protecting and encouraging. And by being so he also attains a state of inner harmony with himself and the world that is often lost in the frenzy of everyday life. This emotional harmony is another fruit of organic gardening, and it is worth all the trouble.

Compost

An organic garden without compost is inconceivable. It is the regular renewal of the earth that makes possible the constant productivity of the soil and the health of the plants. A garden constantly renews itself by recycling its own waste. Humus and nutrients never run out; on the contrary, they are reproduced without interruption. Compost is a very economical crop. Commercial manures and fertilizers for the improvement of the soil are very expensive. The "little dirt factory" in the corner of the garden costs hardly more than a little effort and practical know-how.

In Grandfather's day the art of keeping a compost heap involved a certain amount of effort. The piles of waste lay fallow for at least three years until the last twig was transformed into finely decomposed dirt. And the whole heap had to be carefully turned over once or twice a year.

The rules are somewhat different today. Even organic gardeners keep up with the times if the times promise to provide new and better results. Over the years we have learned that completely decomposed and transformed compost material has lost a portion of its potential nutrient content. Freshly decomposed compost that has been festering for only 6 to 9 months is still rich in microorganisms and valuable components. It does not matter if it is still a little coarse to the touch. The remaining decomposition takes place quickly in the vegetable or flower bed under the protection of a mulch cover. In this way all the nutrients are returned to the soil and to the roots of the plants.

The technical aspects of a compost heap have also been improved. There are containers and specially treated sacks available today that make an efficient preparation of compost possible even in small gardens. Whoever wants to learn the basics of organic gardening can take his or her most important lessons right there where the waste products of the gardening year are once again transformed into earth.

New Life from Mortal Remains

With the falling of the autumn leaves, melancholy begins to slip into the gardener's soul. He cuts off the remains of the last bloom and collects the wilted potato foliage. The yellow tendrils of the bean stalks are removed and the coarse outer leaves of the last head of lettuce are tugged off. Gone. A summer has died. The remains end up on the trash heap.

A gardener who works with nature and understands its deepest secrets really has no reason to bid a sad farewell in the fall. He knows that the compost heap is not a cemetery; nothing of what is decomposed to its smallest particles is ever lost here. Ever new forms of life are re-created from the original building blocks. The organic gardener usually sees no more than the beginning and the end of this miraculous process: the compost heap and the rich earth that results from it. But in the meantime, in the bowels of the compost heap, exciting things are taking place. Billions of tiny microorganisms and innumerable small rodents are silently attacking the dead leaves, twigs, stems, and blades of grass. They are literally tearing them apart.

A well-organized compost area makes the work a lot easier. In the foreground, the pile of gathered garden waste; left, the compost silo; in the middle, some compost heaps; and to the right, receptacles for liquid manures.

In these days of rampant destruction of organic substances, the compost heap produces energy and heat up to 80° C. Only bacteria able to tolerate so much heat can perform this "infernal task." After a few weeks the heap collapses and cools off. Now, as also in the humus layer of the soil, all those animals and microorganisms go to work to rebuild usable substances out of raw materials. This is also the time when the earthworms slink in to perform their particularly valuable service in the building up of new humus.

The brown, fragrant dirt that emerges a few months later is the metabolic product of billions of bacteria, fungi, algae, earthworms, and other small animals. Rose petals, vegetable remains, and blades of grass make their way in and out of the tiny bodies. In the process they are broken down and transformed. They take on a new form in the truest sense of the word. Regardless of how one might want to explain and scientifically elucidate this process, it is still one of the great wonders of our world. It is the external equalizing of life and death, of beginning and end, all of which are closely intertwined. Organic gardeners experience and witness this miracle. The more they understand about it and the more respectfully they treat it, the more visible and ubiquitous will be its positive results.

The Site of the Compost Heap

Since the place where new earth is formed is so very important for the flourishing of the whole garden, it must be carefully chosen. It should be a little out of the way, but still easily

23

Compost

This compost area has paths made of concrete slabs and dividers of railroad ties.

accessible. Most importantly, it should never look like a dark, musty junk pile.

The ideal location would be one protected by hedges or bushes in a warm and partially shaded spot. Drying winds, direct hot sun, and cold

These receptables of stoneware and plastic are good for preparation of liquid manures.

and damp dark corners have a negative effect on the efficiency of the decomposition process.

Organic gardeners are best advised to choose a partially shaded spot that still receives a sufficient amount of warm sunshine. If there are no hedges or bushes nearby, annual plants on climbing structures can serve as good wind screens as well as attractive disguises. A curtain of wicker or an ornamental climbing vine can also be used to separate the compost heap from the rest of the garden. Even a row of tall sunflowers forms an attractive, flowering curtain.

If there is enough space, the compost site should be divided into generous sections. Freedom of movement makes work much easier. Plan on at least two compost heaps and, with flagstones or some other material, build paths about 15″ to 20″ wide between them. This way you will have a solid, tidy foundation that can support the weight of a wheelbarrow heavily laden with refuse. And you will be especially grateful for these paths during rainy weather. You will also need a collection site, which you can fence off with a few planks. This is where all the organic waste is first piled up, cut up, and mixed. Only after there is a sizable heap of material here should the gardener begin the loose stacking of the compost heap.

The ideal compost site should have room enough to include one or more liquid-manure pits and a closed compost container. These containers come in handy all year round for the depositing of kitchen waste. If you do not have this much space, an easily surveyed compost arrangement with several "departments" works well for a larger organic garden. This kind of investment pays off, because it will produce humus and manure all year long at almost no expense.

Of course, not every garden has even this much extra space. Naturally, you will have to be guided by your existing conditions; the following pages are designed to give you many different ideas for building your compost heap. Choose the one that is most appropriate for your needs and space requirements. Experiment to your heart's content until you discover the ideal method for your particular garden. There is only one thing you may not do, and that is to neglect to set up a compost heap.

The Basic Recipe

A compost heap must always be located on uncovered soil. Even silos should not be placed on concrete slabs or on other nonporous materials. Only in the case of closed containers does the surface they rest on have no significance.

Contact with the living earth is important, because this allows the microorganisms and earthworms to wander in and out of the compost heap. When it gets too hot or too cold, these useful creatures can withdraw into the protective depths beneath it.

Moreover, uncovered earth allows for a better regulation of moisture, because it can flow off through the bottom. In dry spells, however, the moisture from the soil can once again be drawn back into the compost heap. Harmonious regulation of moisture is essential for the decomposition processes in the compost heap, and it is

also why the organic gardener should loosen the soil about 4″ to 8″ below the heap as well as under an open silo, leaving a shallow pit. If the garden soil is loamy, this depression should be filled with sand, which will aid in drainage. If the soil is already sandy, the gardener should add a layer of humus-containing material in the shallow pit. This will serve to store up the draining ground water which would otherwise quickly wash away in a sandy soil.

These basics form the lasting foundations of the compost heap. Future

Valuable kitchen waste for the compost heap.

This garbage belongs in the trash can!

Compost

refuse material is then constantly piled up on top and periodically turned over.

All organic substances from the garden can be added to the compost heap: wilted or dead flowers, twigs, potato foliage, pea pods, all sorts of refuse from the vegetable beds, leaves, grass, the trimmings from hedges and fruit trees.

What should not be added to the heap are those parts of plants that are infested with contagious fungus diseases such as clubroot. These remains should be completely destroyed. Pieces of glass, metal, and plastic also have no business on the compost heap. Good organic gardeners always keep two trash cans in their kitchen: The garden can collects all the organic waste of the household, including coffee grounds, tea leaves, dead flowers, vegetable and fruit leftovers, dog and cat hair, and the contents of vacuum-cleaner bags.

Garden waste can be cut up with a spade or a pair of garden shears.

A shredder rapidly transforms unwieldy branches into "predigested" compost material.

Compost

All of these varying substances have to be collected and broken up at the compost site. Branches and flower stems can be cut into 6″–8″ lengths with a sharp knife or hedge clipper. Kitchen waste and the remains from the vegetable beds can be broken up with a spade.

More efficient and quicker are the many forms of commercially available shredders and grinders that are meant for small gardeners. Before buying one, however, it is a good idea to comparison-shop for good quality and capacity. Unfortunately, many followers of the movement jump onto the organic wagon and try to make a quick buck by selling inferior products.

A good shredder or grinder has many advantages for the gardener: Large, thorny piles of compost material can be reduced in no time by running them through the sharp blades of the machine. And it is especially useful for woody waste, which is very valuable for the decomposition process.

The smaller the pieces that finally end up on the compost heap, the sooner they can be decomposed, and the sooner the gardener can reap this most valuable compost crop.

After a goodly amount of refuse has been cut up either by hand or by machine, the gardener should thoroughly mix the various materials together: woody and pliable material, wet leaves and dry sticks. The more even the mix, the more efficient the decomposition.

If too much soft, wet material is heaped together, a lack of oxygen and a resulting putrefaction can easily occur. But if too much woody waste is

For even decomposition, damp and dry materials should be thoroughly mixed together.

piled up, the compost remains dry and sterile.

Always add rather large amounts of compost at a time—at least 18″ to 24″. Thin layers do not warm up. The first phase of decomposition must proceed quickly and at a high temperature.

The innumerable creatures that live in the ground and that transform the garden waste into new dirt need a sufficient amount of oxygen, moisture, warmth, and "hard-labor rations" in the form of nitrogen. A good proportion of nitrogen is usually contained in fresh green refuse. But the composition of the compost material is constantly changing. For this reason organic gardeners should mix a little organic manure in with the compost

Compost

material, just to be on the safe side. By adding this, they keep their invisible workers on their toes. Where there is not enough nitrogen, the rate of decomposition is also slowed down.

Organic gardeners should note the following important rules for an efficient compost heap:

Air must be able to circulate freely among the compost material. It is vital for the animals and microbes that work "underground." This is why the material has to be kept loosely mixed and be exposed to the air.

Moisture is another element vital to the life of the animals and the microbes, but it has to be distributed evenly. Standing puddles produce putrefaction. If the compost is too dry, essential creatures tend to wander away. Organic gardeners should therefore water their compost heap during hot weather. During prolonged periods of rain, however, they should protect the heap from too much moisture by covering it.

Heat accelerates decomposition; if the air is tempered, the process moves from the outside in. Moreover, heat is produced by the breakdown process within the heap. A protected location and a covering of grass, hay, or leaves helps to keep the warmth in the heap.

If an organic gardener follows these important basic rules, he or she will soon know the art of composting. You have to work at it with heart and hand, which includes observing carefully and acting at the right moment. The compost heap is a living, breathing organism. If the organic gardener remembers that this is where the brown material upon which we all depend originates, then it is certainly worth the effort.

The Compost Heap

The "classic" shape of a compost heap has been developed and maintained over generations. The finished heap is an elongated structure resembling a low tent, between 5' and 6' long, and 2' wide. The height depends upon individual garden conditions, but a freshly constructed heap should not be taller than 4½' or 5'.

These dimensions have proven to be the best, for here compost material can be easily manipulated. If you pile it too high, you have to contend with the fact that the pressure of the material leads to clumping on the bottom and a lack of oxygen.

Organic refuse accumulates only slowly and one rarely has enough to make a heap at the start. This is why it is best to begin with a surface of about 8 square feet, so that you can add to the top. Later on you can always widen the pile as the need arises.

Ideally, the lowest level should be composed of dry, coarse material such as cuttings from trees. This foundation helps ventilate the heap and drain off the water. On top of this you can pile about 8" of mixed refuse, followed by a sprinkling of a little additive as needed to help in the decomposition process. These additives include:

Lime that has been pulverized to the consistency of powdered sugar. The most recommended form is ground dolomitic limestone.

Organic Manure, which stimulates the microorganisms to intense activity. Any fertilizer that contains nitrogen is good for this purpose: horn meal, dry-blood meal, dried barnyard

How to build a compost heap: In the foreground, the bottom of the heap composed of coarse material; in the background, the first layer sprinkled with earth, stone meal, or a compost starter.

The finished heap is covered with a layer of hay. Other suitable materials are leaves, grass, or old sacks.

manure, or guano. You can also pour nitrogen-containing liquid manure made from stinging nettles over the pile.

Peat Moss can be scattered sparingly between the layers. This expanding natural product absorbs excess moisture and retains the valuable nitrogen produced by the microorganisms during the decomposition process. In poorly constructed compost heaps, this valuable plant nutrient frequently dissipates into the air without ever being used.

Dirt which is rich in humus and somewhat loamy serves the same good purpose as commercial peat moss. Simply strew a few shovelfuls of good garden soil between the individual layers of the compost heap. Actually, some humus is always present in compost; it is brought in, for example, on the roots of plants along with the clinging dirt.

A Compost Starter can be purchased in a garden center. There are many different kinds, however. They con-

tain, among other things, peat moss, nitrogen, plant and bulbous extracts, and ground bacteria in dried form. These ingredients stimulate the life in the soil and thus accelerate decomposition. Preparations of this kind are highly recommended for beginning organic gardeners because they have a positive effect on the production of compost and thus help assure the success of the undertaking.

Ripe Compost replaces many other additives. It is teeming with natural ground life which quickly conquers the well-mixed refuse. Moreover, compost soil contains nutrients and is capable of absorbing moisture. Advanced organic gardeners who always have a good supply of ripe compost on hand use this homemade starter for stimulating their new heaps. It is inexpensive and top-quality.

After you have set up the first layer and sprinkled it with the selected additives, you should follow the same procedure to build up one layer after another. The heap should taper off at

Neighbors like this one are rare: The farmer is bringing manure from his barn.

the top, and the sides should slope outward to a certain extent. This is what gives it its tentlike appearance.

Finally, the compost heap should be covered with a protective coat of loosely arranged organic material such as hay, cut grass, or leaves. You can also use old burlap sacks or grass mats. This covering keeps the compost warm and moist, and also protects it against driving storms. Only in prolonged periods of rain should a temporary plastic covering be placed over the heap so that it does not get too wet and thus putrefy.

And finally one last tip: Remove weeds whenever necessary before they go to seed. If this cannot be done on time, collect these plants separately and bury them in the middle of a freshly built compost heap. Diseased leaves and fruits also ought to be stored there. Only severe cases of fungus diseases like clubroot should be very carefully isolated from the rest of the material. The greatest heat develops in the middle of the heap, and this serves to kill the disease carriers and the germinating ability of seeds. The only prerequisite for this, of course, is an efficient and constant rate of decomposition with temperatures of at least 50°–70° C.

There is no need to shift or turn over

Dung should have its own heap and be sprinkled only with earth or clay meal.

The completed manure heap is covered over with earth. Never use lime!

Compost

small, loosely constructed compost heaps. The material will have turned to dirt in about 9 months. Larger heaps should be turned over at least once so that the top becomes the bottom and the bottom the top. In this way air can once again penetrate the mass and accelerate the decomposition.

Compost heaps that have been poorly constructed for whatever reason have to be taken apart and rebuilt. Damp, rotting substances are best left lying in the open air for a few days so that they can dry out. Only then may they be remixed into the rest of the compost material.

Always build your compost heap on the same spot. The remains of the old heap lying on the ground form a positive source of "infection" which is easily and quickly transferable to new piles of refuse.

Open or closed silos keep the waste-collection area neat and clean.

Compost Silos

Containers in which compost material can be stored are practical and neat. They represent a good way, especially in small gardens, to produce the valuable humus in the least amount of space. Handy and skilled organic gardeners can make their own containers out of wooden planks or wire screening. Many useful models made of a variety of materials are commercially available, such as closed compost pails and a thermal model which retains the heat particularly well because it is lined with styrofoam. The compost should be layered in a silo or closed container just as carefully as in an open heap. Many models have an opening at the top where new compost material can be added and

another at the bottom so that the processed dirt can be shoveled out.

Compost Sacks

Special plastic sacks equipped with air holes are also available and are particularly well suited for recycling organic waste in even the smallest garden. Since the capacity of these sacks is very limited, it is essential that the compost material be broken up and mixed as thoroughly as possible. Also, since there is no contact with the living ground, the organic gardener himself has to provide the microorganisms. A nursery or garden center sells compost starters with dried ground bacteria for these sacks. Moisture is best added very carefully with a watering can. The sacks should be shaken rather frequently to ensure that air continuously penetrates amid

Compost

Compost in a sack: New soil is created in special sacks filled with well-shredded garden waste or grass and sawdust.

and between the decomposing substances. Once the sacks are filled, they can simply be placed in the shade under a bush or shrub until the compost is ripe. If done correctly, this may be a matter of only a few months.

Lawn Compost

Freshly mown, moist grass presents a tremendous problem, and many gardeners have had some rather foul-smelling experiences with it. The green blades contain a great deal of moisture and rapidly form nonporous, dripping-wet layers that immediately begin to putrefy.

In order to remedy this evil and make the best use of this often very quickly accumulating organic material, experienced gardeners need only resort to the opposite extreme: Mix very dry material in with the freshly mown wet grass. Small wood chips or sawdust are very good for this purpose.

Both ingredients have to be mixed together thoroughly. You might also throw in a bit of compost starter and some peat moss before putting it all in a compost sack. Remember to place these sacks under a bush or in a partially shady corner and shake them vigorously from time to time. This special mixture decomposes very rapidly. If weather conditions are favorable, organic gardeners can reap coarse mulching compost from the sack in about 6 weeks and can then distribute it throughout the garden.

Surface Compost

This is the simplest method of transforming organic substances into new

Compost

soil, and it requires neither a compost heap nor a container. Broken-up waste materials or a bumper crop of fallen autumn leaves can be spread over open beds or tree roots in a loose and not very deep layer.

In the fall organic gardeners can add a little fertilizer, compost starter, or semiripe mulching material on top of this layer of leaves. The whole mixture should be worked slightly with a hoe so that some contact with the earth is established. The rest is then taken care of by the microorganisms which quickly invade this inviting scene. They decompose the organic substances and transform them on the spot into nutrient-containing humus. This type of compost is actually only another variation of mulching, and it is particularly useful around tree trunks, harvested vegetable beds, and the open areas under bushes and shrubs.

Compost can be formed on the spot from a leaf cover on already harvested beds. The light leaves can be weighted down with coarse compost.

Mighty Assistants: Shredders and Grinders

These machines were produced with home gardens in mind and are usually sold in a price range comparable to that of lawn mowers. Such a machine is a worthwhile investment for a large garden that produces substantial amounts of waste that need to be reduced rapidly. These machines also have their place in smaller gardens and soon pay for themselves simply by accelerating the decomposition of finely ground material. Organic gardeners thus reap what is frequently their best soil-improver, their own compost, in a very short time, and this can save time and money.

Compost

Waste materials that have been reduced in a shredder decompose rapidly and evenly.

Ripe compost should be spread evenly over the bed and raked in only superficially.

Application

Regardless of the method used to produce compost, the day will come when the organic gardener reaps his or her first crop of fragrant brown humus. It is now ready to be loaded onto a wheelbarrow and transported to wherever it is most needed.

The surface of the area to be covered with compost should be carefully prepared beforehand and the ground should be thoroughly weeded and loosened. The earth should always be moist when you spread compost, and this is why it is best to do it on a cloudy day so that the precious humus does not dry out.

Spread the compost over the surface in a layer about 2 fingers deep and rake it in very lightly. This living earth should never be buried! The final step is to spread a mulch cover of leaves, grass, or pulverized waste material over the compost. This keeps it moist, warm and alive and at the same time provides a well-ventilated cover that does its work during the winter. By the time spring returns, the greater part of it, too, will have been transformed into rich, new soil. The remains of the mulch cover should not be removed until it is time to seed or plant. The gardener will discover in this loose humus an ideal matrix for a future vegetable bed.

Mulching

Mulching means simply covering the ground. This is one of the most important procedures in a natural garden. Leaf, hay, and grass covers have become the distinguishing characteristic of all organic gardens.

For many gardeners, the concept of mulching signifies a painful rejection of cherished habits. Anyone used to priding himself on his tidy garden, beaming over immaculately raked, empty brown beds in fall has to change his whole way of thinking. But once the initial resistance is overcome, it is not so difficult. Most people admire the glorious colors of the leaf cover as they rustle through the fallen foliage during the autumnal walk in the forest. Isn't it just as beautiful when the leaves lie under the bushes in one's own garden all winter long? The world looks exactly the way we want to see it. If we have a kindly outlook, the world gives a cheerful reflection. If we have a suspicious eye, our surroundings seem gloomy. Organic gardeners need make only a slight adjustment in the way they look at things, and they will soon discover that even mulched beds can be a pleasant sight.

Naked Ground Is Unnatural

Nature never voluntarily strips itself. Wherever the naked earth has been exposed as a result of an act of God, animals, or man, nature hastens to provide a green covering as soon as possible, and it doesn't take long before grasses and weeds start to spring up again. Very soon the brown skin of the earth is no longer visible; it

Wild plants covering construction sites.

is once again covered as well as protected.

This process has nothing to do with prudishness or with aesthetics: It is merely an act of survival that has been practiced for millennia. The humus layer is sensitive and fragile. Thousands of plant roots crisscross through it in an underground network and hold the precious crumbs tightly between their strands and filaments. Their foliage then serves to protect the earth from wind and sun, both of which threaten the vital moisture content. The thick leaf covering on the forest floor serves this same purpose.

If the humus layer anywhere on earth should be left open and unprotected, exposed to the heavens as a result of some human act or natural disaster, its fate is as good as sealed. Downpours float the topsoil away. The sun dries it out. The wind blows the dust far and wide. Finally, all that is

Mulching

left are bare cliffs or arid wasteland steppes. The possibility of a natural regeneration is lost forever.

Many a previously fertile area has been thus transformed by an exploitative lumbering operation or by other catastrophes into an inviable wilderness. Organic gardeners need only visualize such a scene if they still find it difficult to abandon that scoured and polished vegetable and flower bed. Naked earth is always unnatural and, in the long run, disastrous.

The Material for Warm Covers

Garden soil, too, dries out quickly if it is left unprotected against the rays of the sun or the ravages of the wind. If the soil is sandy, there is the additional danger that a part of the surface will be blown away. Heavy soils rich in lime bake in the hot summer sun until they resemble clay roofing tiles. Moreover, violent downpours need only minutes to disintegrate the fine, crumbly structure of humus. The patient work of the gardener as well as of innumerable small animals and microorganisms is once again reduced to naught.

Organic gardeners can prevent all of this if they cover every inch of exposed soil in their garden by following the model nature provides. By doing this they protect not only the precious humus but billions of useful microorganisms, which need moisture and warmth for their work, as well.

The material needed for this vital, warm covering can usually be found in the garden. Organic gardeners can

A leaf cover is good for strawberry patches.

Always available: grass as a ground cover.

Mulching

use mown grass, leaves, or simply broken-up weeds. Hay or straw can also be used for the cultivation of many different plants. Sawdust and pulverized tree bark provide special mulches.

Mulch covers are spread over harvested vegetable beds, on top of tree roots, under berry bushes, between shrubs, and underneath ornamental trees and shrubs. This organic material should form a loose and porous covering. It is better to spread thin layers, 6″ deep at the most, than to pile up high mountains of refuse. If the covering is too thick, the underlying soil soon suffers from a lack of oxygen and begins to decay. In addition, dark, wet areas develop, which attract slugs. These voracious creatures then settle in the middle of the bed and do a great deal of damage.

Spreading new mulch covers at regular intervals offers these advantages:

- The ground under the cover remains warm and moist.
- The microorganisms in the ground are well nourished and productive.
- The ground is neither washed away by rain nor baked by the sun. It remains loose and crumbly.
- Weeds have difficulty in penetrating through the cover and can be easily removed.
- Plants thrive in the well-balanced growing conditions of mulched beds.
- There is much less need for watering, hoeing, and weeding.
- Fertile humus regenerates itself because the mulch material is constantly being transformed into new soil.

Woody garden waste decomposes slowly.

Living Carpets

You cannot spread mulch everywhere in the garden. Despite all the ecological advantages, it can have a disturbing effect in an ornamental garden. In such places organic gardeners ought to follow nature's example and let the ground cover itself with low bushes and grasses. These durable plants are also called "ground covers" by those in the know.

These living knotted carpets are beautiful between roses, ornamental shrubs, and wild bushes. The plants' dense growth soon unites them all, and they then protect the earth much as a natural mulch layer or plant cover does.

Mulching

Reputable nurseries and garden centers offer a large selection of these plants. There are carpet bushes for sunny and for shady locations. When making your choice, however, you should keep in mind that vigorous growth is dependent upon the proper location of the plant.

There are also several plants that are appropriate for a vegetable garden and they, too, form a living ground cover for a period of time. These include, among others, mustard seed, which germinates as quickly as cress. In only a few days it forms a thick green cover on harvested beds. The innumerable fine roots of the mustard plant loosen up the earth, and after a short while the leaves can either be mown down or they freeze back by themselves in the fall. The rest remains on the bed throughout the winter as a mulch cover. There are even several species among the legumes or papilionaceous plants that are well suited for sowing in the garden. Organic gardeners can use these useful plants, too, to cover a bed for a period of time. Very good for this purpose are the various species of clover

Low shrubs, such as knotgrass *(Polygonum)* and pennycress *(Thlaspi arvense)* , join to make a lasting ground cover.

Spadework? No Thanks!

and lupine. These plants not only serve as a living mulch carpet, but they also fertilize and regenerate the soil. You can read more about that in the section entitled "Green Fertilizers" (p. 46).

In many gardens, late autumn is the season of spadework and backaches. A belief that stems from Grandfather's day maintains that the earth is supposed to hibernate in the form of coarse brown clods. Instead of incurring the aches and pains that go along with getting the earth into this shape, organic gardeners ought to spend an hour sitting on a garden bench. While the last rays of the autumn sun warm their rested and relaxed backs, they may well pass the time in quiet reflection.

We have already learned that the humus layer consists of 2 carefully constructed "stories." During the course of an entire garden year, gardeners have made great efforts to protect and nourish this complicated but well-organized world. Should they now sink a sharp iron blade into this soil teeming with life and expose this underground world piecemeal to the open air?

The more an organic gardener thinks about this, the more illogical it seems. The different layers of the soil will be turned topsy-turvy with every stab of the spade. The oxygen-loving microorganisms of the upper layer will end up in the airless depths. The creatures of the lower layer will suddenly find themselves under open skies. The order that was so laboriously established will be completely undone, and it will be a long time before the bil-

The old-fashioned way to loosen the soil.

lions of "little elves" find their places again and reestablish the old, accustomed state. What's the use of all this?

"The most important thing is frost-friability" is the reply the traditional green thumbs give the optimistic organic gardener. "Especially heavy soils should freeze in the winter so that they fall apart in small clumps in the spring."

An attentive nature observer can refute this argument as soon as the strong spring rains begin to fall. The friable, frozen clods of earth are soon smashed by the driving downpours, the ground turns to mud, and on the next sunny day it bakes together as solid as ever before.

So what was the use of that autumnal chaos? It certainly did not benefit the life of the soil. And as far as the formation of friable clods is concerned, it had at best a very short-lived effect.

Garden forks loosen the soil.

Caring for the Soil Without a Spade

The leisurely hour our organic gardener spent in quiet reflection on his bench profited him more than any laborious efforts to move the earth. From now on he is perfectly clear about one thing at least: Spadework? No thanks! He uses his head and spares his back. Moreover, he leaves the digging to those who really know how to do it—the earthworms.

Following this fundamental decision, of course, even in a well-tended organic garden, preparations for the winter have to be made. All open spaces in ornamental as well as kitchen gardens must be loosened so that the soil remains porous to air and water. This task calls for a pitchfork, which should be driven into the ground and rocked back and forth a few times. In this manner organic gardeners can work their way piece by piece through the garden. The earth

has now been loosened without disturbing or reversing the various layers. Another very useful tool for working the earth is a "sowing sickle." This instrument was especially designed for an organic garden. It consists of a sickle-shaped prong that can be easily drawn through the soil. This "sowing sickle," too, loosens the ground without disturbing or destroying the layers.

The final step once again involves spreading an organic fertilizer wherever necessary for crop rotation. Each bed should be treated with compost and covered with a warm mulch. The ground bacteria will continue working for a long time beneath this warm cover. They will increase the humus and tend the friable soil—better than any spade, more lastingly than the deepest frost. Even the spring rains cannot harm this loose humus structure. The heavy raindrops will be distributed evenly over the soft mulch cover. Their ferocity spent, they will trickle into the earth in the form of beneficial moisture. In the meantime our reassured organic gardeners can plan on a creative winter pause. Their backs do not ache, and their gardens are in the best of hands.

The Earthworm

Organic gardeners should use the peaceful winter weeks to increase their knowledge of nature. As a matter of fact, the earthworm is a creature worthy of a closer look. By next spring the gardener will have come to appreciate this inconspicuous but indispensable co-worker all the more.

The large grayish-brown earth-

Spadework? No Thanks!

worms (Lumbricus terrestris) are the living spades of every organic garden. They can dig down to a depth of several feet, and the tubelike tunnels they leave behind create hollow spaces that aerate the soil and distribute moisture. Even the roots of plants like to follow these underground passages, for they are lined with the finest humus and richest nutrients.

Little muckworms (Eisenia foetida), on the other hand, make themselves useful in the compost heap. They love moisture, warmth, and an abundance of organic waste.

All earthworms spend their lives eating dirt and dying parts of plants such as bits of root or wilted leaves. Their elongated bodies resemble a single intestinal canal, whose function is to combine organic substances with the mineral constituents of the earth and the digestive secretions of the worms. These tireless cultivators of the soil deposit little piles of humus which contain high concentrations of nutrients. Examinations of earthworm excretions have found an average of 7 times as much nitrogen, 3 times as much potash, twice as much phosphorus, and 6 times as much magnesium as is present in the surrounding soil.

Earthworms are thus not only excellent soil-looseners but also valuable fertilizing agents. In good soils these helpful little assistants congregate in great numbers. If one were to collect the earthworms in 2½ acres (one hectare) of good, arable soil, their combined weight, it has been estimated, would equal that of an average-sized cow. This underground "herd" converts 70 times its own weight into nutrient-rich humus every year.

Statistics such as these demonstrate that in the course of time these inconspicuous creatures achieve enormous results. They contribute a great deal to the fertility of the soil, and the only wages they demand for these services are good living conditions.

The mulch covers that have been spread all over the natural garden provide the earthworms with a sumptuous feast. These creatures find the

A simple experiment reveals the work of the earthworm. Fill two containers half with sand, half with dirt. Add some earthworms to the right container and provide them with some organic waste for food. Result: mixed, loose layers and a clear increase of humus.

Fertilizers and Their Use

humid atmosphere beneath this organic waste very much to their liking. If an organic gardener should push the leaves aside one early evening, he would unearth innumerable worms. They will spend the rest of their days producing high-quality natural manure.

All plants need nourishment to grow. The natural cycle proceeds undisturbed in the wilderness, but garden plants are no longer able to care for themselves, as it were. They have been "overcultivated" by mankind for centuries. The cabbages and their relatives that we know today are much bigger and leafier than their ancestor, the wild cabbage on the coasts of the Atlantic. We have been spoiled by the overabundant harvests of our apple and cherry orchards, for they far outstrip the production of the wild crabapple or the bird-cherry trees.

To produce these abundant harvests, plants need rich nourishment. They are dependent upon the care of the gardener, who must see to it that they are constantly replenished. Lasting productivity is inconceivable in an organic garden without a reasonable program of fertilization.

Nourishment for Ground Organisms and Plant Roots

Every year plants absorb a portion of their nourishment from the soil. If healthy, vigorous plants are to flourish in the same spot the following spring, exhausted nutrients have to be replaced. In an organic garden, how-

ever, the gardener does not feed the roots directly, but only via the soil.

Even the beginning gardener has realized by now that the countless creatures living in the humus layer of the soil are capable of constantly producing nutrients. These natural products have the advantage of being absorbed by root systems in controlled portions according to the plant's need. In well-tended soil, moreover, the number of nutrients is varied and balanced. One might be tempted to say that it consists of a healthy, mixed diet. Commercial fertilizers in the form of salts, on the other hand, penetrate directly to the roots via easily absorbable water solutions. The greatest danger of this type of fertilization lies in the fact that the plants absorb too much of this beneficial brew and that the rest is very quickly flushed into the deeper depths. Organic nourishment, produced by microorganisms, on the other hand, is readily storable. These creatures, as well as the humus itself, hold on to it until it is really needed.

The basic source of nourishment in an organic garden is naturally the compost. But poor soils and plants with strong appetites need additional food for strength above and beyond this. To meet this need, organic gardeners turn to the so-called organic fertilizers. The immediate purpose of these materials is to provide food for the microorganisms, which then transform the useful ingredients into appropriate "plant-friendly" substances. Such an underground food production from without develops slowly and continuously, and thus helps avoid an accelerated, artificially stimulated growth.

Fertilizers

Manure can be spread as a loose ground cover; it decomposes over the winter.

you must add those specific organic fertilizers that contain the missing element in larger amounts. If a garden is regularly tended with compost for a long period of time, these imbalance deficiencies hardly ever pose a problem. In new gardens or in poor soils, however, a lack of potash, phosphorus, or nitrogen can pose serious problems for the gardener. He or she can obtain more detailed information about the state of the soil merely by sending a soil sample to be analyzed by an appropriate testing institution, which may be a private or a state-affiliated establishment.

The nourishment needs of individual plant species vary greatly. The nutrient content of different fertilizers varies as well. This is why organic gardeners ought to familiarize themselves with the most important fundamentals of fertilizing, and for this they need to know a little chemistry as well!

Carbon, oxygen, and hydrogen are the basic elements that plants can absorb for themselves from the air and the soil. The fundamental nutrients nitrogen (N), phosphorus (P), and potash (K) have to be added. These are called NPK fertilizers in keeping with their chemical composition. In addition, trace elements and lime are essential for the healthy growth of plant life.

If the soil lacks one of the main nutrients, the plants suffer from symptoms of malnutrition. In such cases

Animal Fertilizers

Even "natural" fertilizers should not be applied indiscriminately. Responsible organic gardeners should learn the quality and composition of the most important sources of organic nutrients so that they can apply them with pinpoint precision.

The waste products of various house pets have long been among the proven natural fertilizers. It is better not to use them "raw," but rather via the detour of the compost heap. They then fertilize in a milder and more compatible way.

Dung compost should always be applied separately, and lime should never be used in combination with it. This otherwise valuable ingredient releases the essential nitrogen in dung compost, and the released nitrogen then dissipates into the air in the form of ammonia. Always apply dung in layers with ripe compost or peat moss.

Cow Manure, fresh and full of straw,

Fertilizers and Their Use

is a mild, balanced dung that contains all the important nutrients.

Dried Cow Manure is equally recommended, but should come from a reputable and impeccable livestock source. "California Cow Manure," for example, is of high quality and is especially rich in potash. This particular nutrient is present in only small amounts in most organic manures.

Horse Manure is just about as rich in nutrients as cow dung, but it produces a lot of heat in the soil. This manure is good for warming purposes in hotbeds. When used as a fertilizer, it should be combined with compost.

Pig Manure contains mostly potash and nitrogen, and it is one of the cold manures.

Sheep, Goat, and Rabbit Manures are high in nitrogen. They have a warming effect and can cause burns on plants. These manures should be mixed with compost.

Bird Dungs are particularly rich in phosphorus, but they also contain a lot of potash and nitrogen. These manures may come from chickens, pigeons, or sea birds (guano); they have a very high warming effect, penetrate into the soil more quickly than other manures, and can therefore cause burns and vigorously rank growth. These manures are best applied in the form of liquid and then only in diluted concentrations.

Horn Meal, Blood Meal and Bone Meal are also sources of animal manure. They originate as slaughterhouse by-products and can be bought in the form of commercial mixtures. Here, too, it is important to control the quality. One recommended product, for example, is guaranteed to contain no hide meal and is therefore free of

dangerous heavy-metal sediments like chromium.

Horn-meal fertilizers primarily contain nitrogen and phosphorus; bone meal is especially rich in phosphorus; and blood meal has a particularly high nitrogen content. All three together provide a "complete organic fertilizer" which release its nutrients slowly over an extended period of time.

Liquid Plant Manures

Plants, too, can provide the raw material for excellent manures. They can be mixed in water and left to ferment; this produces natural nutrient-containing solutions that are tolerated well by most garden plants. One great advantage of this type of homemade plant food is that it is extraordinarily economical, for most of the ingredients can be gleaned from nature without cost.

Organic gardeners ought to try the liquid manure brewed from stinging nettles. Over the years this fertilizer has become one of the proven components of natural plant care.

Stinging-Nettle Liquid Manure

To produce this liquid fertilizer you will need a rather large container about the size of a barrel, an old stoneware crock, or a plastic pail. Metal containers should not be used. Place a goodly amount of freshly cut stinging nettles in the container. Both the large and the small varieties (*Urtica dioica* and *Urtica urens*) are suitable just as long as the plants have not yet gone to seed. Fill the container to the top with water—rainwater, if at all possible. Leave about a hand's

Fertilizers and Their Use

breadth free beneath the rim, since this brew produces a high foam during the fermentation period.

Using a stick, stir the mixture vigorously once a day so that the oxygen can react with the rapidly beginning decomposition process. Finally, place a wire or plastic screen over the top so that no animal or pet can inadvertently fall into the brew and drown.

This concoction ferments particularly rapidly in a sunny, warm location. However, it also produces unpleasant odors which may be a source of irritation to your neighbors. To avoid this you can sprinkle a few handfuls of stone meal over the liquid or stir in a few drops of valerian-flower extract. Both of these help retard the stench. After 2 weeks or so, the liquid will begin to settle and the fermentation subside. The manure is now ready for use and can be covered with a lid while stored in the container.

As a liquid garden manure, this stinging-nettle solution should be diluted with 1 part solution to 10 parts water, and poured directly over the roots of the plants. It serves as a very good additive for plants that need a great deal of nourishment, like tomatoes, cabbage, celery, cucumbers, and leeks. Beans, peas, and onions. on the other hand, should not be fertilized with this solution!

A dose of liquid manure is highly recommended for annual summer flowers, shrubs, roses, berry bushes, and fruit trees.

After just a few days observant organic gardeners will notice the results of this stinging-nettle soup: The plants will start to set dark green leaves; they will grow visibly while still remaining squat and vigorous. This is

due, among other things, to the nitrogen content of this form of manure.

Stinging nettles possess other good qualities which render the fertilized plants more vigorous and more resistant. These phenomena have not been fully researched as yet, but every gardener can experience these positive results in his or her own garden.

Other medicinal herbs can be added to enrich or alter the liquid manure you have just made from stinging net-

Various receptacles used for liquid manures: a stinging-nettle manure, male-form manure, and comfrey manure. Below: ripe liquid manure.

Lupines are nitrogen collectors.

tles. For instance, you can mix in a few handfuls of horsetail, comfrey, chives, or onions with the nettles. Even a handful of animal dung or a spadeful of ripe compost can round out this nutritious plant food. The number of possible experiments depends solely upon your degree of experience. As long as you stay on nature's trail, your garden will thank you for it.

Nitrogen nodules on bean roots.

Green Fertilizers

Plants themselves fertilize the garden, too, and not only by means of liquid manure, but also directly in the beds. Legumes as well as papilionaceous plants rank among the best of these good, on-the-spot soil-improvers.

These green specialists work together with certain types of bacteria to form nitrogen-containing nodules on their roots. These so-called nodule bacteria promote the welfare of the plant, which thus possesses its own fertilizer factory, as it were; however, they also improve the surrounding soil, which absorbs that portion of nitrogen that tends to spill over.

Plants that produce this valuable green fertilizer include, among others, clover, vetch, and lupine. The papilionaceous plants of the vegetable garden can also be added to this list: peas, beans, and soybeans. Gardeners should sow these plants in beds whose nitrogen content has already been partially consumed by nutrient-demanding plants, for the legumes will then replenish the soil with nitrogen. The other plants that produce green fertilizers should be sown in already harvested beds to help the soil recover its lost strength. Their widespread root masses collect nutrients, but at the same time their expansive and deep root systems help loosen the earth. Legumes perform yeoman's duty in hard-packed construction sites or in fallow land that is meant to be transformed into a garden.

The luxuriant above-ground foliage should be mowed down and later used as mulch or compost material. As many roots as possible should

Fertilizers and Their Use

remain in the ground, where they leave nutrients as well as loose cavities and hollows in the wake of their decomposition. Organic gardeners can purchase various papilionaceous plants in nurseries or garden centers; prepared mixtures in convenient quantities are also available.

Inorganic Fertilizers

To most organic gardeners, the designation "inorganic fertilizer" is a provocation. They understand it to mean nothing more than synthetic commercial salts. All too frequently, however, they forget that nature itself is one of the major salt and mineral producers of the world.

Open-minded organic gardeners ought at least to know that there are also natural inorganic fertilizers which can be used for specific purposes in specific cases without deviating from the narrow paths of natural cultivation.

Crude Phosphates are found in ancient deposits that originated from the bones and teeth of prehistoric animals. Today this product, which has been chemically transformed by nature itself, is worked and sold in a pulverized form. "Hyperphos" *Superphos*phate decomposes slowly and is also good for organic gardens.

Basic Slag is a natural by-product of iron smelting. The ground cinders (slag) contain phosphorus, manganese, and lime, and these elements are released by the microorganisms in the soil.

Potash Magnesia Sulfate is another by-product of mining operations. It originated in the salt deposits of pre-

historic seas. The most important consideration here is to choose a potassium product that is poor in salt so that it can be used to treat acute potash deficiencies as quickly as possible.

All of these natural inorganic fertilizers should be used only to alleviate a definite nutrient deficiency. After several years of organic garden and soil care, such direct methods as these are usually no longer necessary because the nutrient content of the soil will have become sufficiently balanced.

Stone Meals

In addition to the above-mentioned fertilizers, there are preparations aimed at soil improvement. They heighten the quality of the humus without increasing the proportion of other nutrients already present in sufficient quantities. Among the most important of these natural means of fertilization are the stone meals.

These finely pulverized stone dusts are produced as a waste product in quarries and in the stone-working

Stone meal improves the quality of the soil.

Fertilizers and Their Use

industry. The composition varies according to the stone from which the powder originates. Primitive rock meal, for instance, is obtained from granite or basalt. High in lime content are those stone meals that come from magnesium carbonate. Common to all stone meals is a high proportion of important trace elements and minerals.

The clay meals have a special characteristic: They are extraordinarily expansive and can absorb enormous amounts of water. Sandy soils particularly can be improved by the addition of clay meals.

Organic gardeners cannot go wrong with either of these types, for such preparations contribute greatly to the improvement of the structure of the soil if they are used regularly. One could almost say they work like a savings bank in the ground. Water and nutrients can be stored very efficiently there. With the help of microorganisms, the vital elements are then prepared and slowly distributed to the plant roots according to need. Even the valuable humus substances are increased and the crumbly structure of the humus layer remains constant wherever a gardener regularly applies stone meal.

In every case, however, the organic gardener should pay close attention to the varying composition of these stone meals. Calcareous products, for instance, should be used only where the soil needs additional doses of lime.

Lime

Lime is another of the soil-improvers. However, it should be used only when targeted to a specific purpose. This is why every organic gardener should be well informed about the characteristics of this natural mineral. Limestone unlocks nutrients and improves the crumbly structure of the soil. Above all, however, it fixes acids. Acidic soils, then, can attain plant-friendly levels ranging between slightly acidic and neutral with the help of a dose of limestone. An excessive application of lime is always dangerous, for the soil tends to respond with a strong alkaline reaction. Once attained, this unfavorable alteration in the soil can be undone only with great difficulty and does great damage to the plants.

In every instance organic gardeners should heed the old farmer's maxim: Lime makes rich fathers and poor sons. This means that a vigorous fertilization program with lime-containing manures can have an initially strong and positive effect on the growth of the plants, but the end result is frequently the rapid depletion of humus. Smart gardeners will therefore use lime only in moderation and for very specific and targeted purposes. Sandy soils are usually deficient in lime, but they are unable to tolerate strong doses of it at any one time. Loamy soils usually have a sufficiently high lime content. Organic gardeners can stay on the safe side if they constantly add small doses of lime to their garden by mixing it with compost. Living, healthy humus usually does not suffer from a deficiency of this important mineral. When in times of transition the soil needs a substantial amount of outside help, the use of calcareous stone meal or dolomitic limestone products is highly recommended.

Bountiful harvests are the natural result of organic methods of soil care and fertilizinq.

Information about the lime content of the soil can be attained easily and relatively reliably from soil tests done in glass test tubes. Lime-analyzers like this can be purchased in just about any garden center.

Peat

The light brown substratum of marshy bogs has been highly touted as a panacea for the garden. The increasing demand for it threatens our few remaining marshlands and in many cases contributes but little to the improvement of the garden. Peat possesses the good quality of being able to absorb and store a lot of water. It can therefore regulate the moisture content of the soil. Employing this substratum is sometimes appropriate for the structural improvement of sandy soils. In wet, loamy soils peat can be used to consolidate superfluous moisture to a certain extent.

Nevertheless, there is one thing an organic gardener must know: An excessive use of peat turns the soil acidic. This fibrous substratum of "mummified" plants is by nature totally lacking in nutrients, and this is why commercially prepared peat moss is enriched with synthetic salts. Since organic gardeners are nature

Crop Rotation and Mixed Planting

conservationists as well, they should use this product of the bogs only sparingly and for specific targeted purposes—for example, around plants that need acidic soil, such as azaleas, heather, or hydrangeas. There are more lasting and more environmentally friendly ways to improve the soil structure and its water content, including the use of compost, stone meal, and mulch covers. "Fertilizing" with peat moss means an unnecessary exploitation of nature. The many other materials described in this chapter serve the organic gardener as equally good sources of nutrients for the soil.

Constant crop rotation should be the motto of organic gardeners when they sit down to plan their garden. Like that of the ground covers and the regeneration of humus via compost, this axiom, too, grows out of the careful observation of nature. An obser-

The colorful profusion of a kitchen garden rewards the efforts of mixed plantings.

Crop Rotation and Mixed Planting

vant organic gardener will never find monotonous stretches of one single plant in an open meadow; monocultures like pure spruce forests or enormous wheat fields are always signs of an artificial world created by the hand of man.

Nature prefers communities of mixed plants. These highly diversified neighborhoods have many advantages, not the least of which is the fact that different plants make different claims on the soil. Each one takes from it only the nutrients it needs and leaves the rest for the others. Moreover, the plants themselves use their roots to deposit substances that affect the composition of the humus layer. The greater the variety of plants, the greater the variety of organic substances that enrich the ground and regenerate the soil. This also helps prevent an unbalanced extraction of essential nutrients.

Farmers have known these principles for centuries and have acted in keeping with them. Every year they rotated the crop in a particular field. After three years of successive cultivation, they left the field fallow for one. The earth then recuperated with the help of beneficial wild flowers and weeds.

If this natural system of fluctuation and the lessons of traditional agricultural procedures are carried over into the home garden, the foundations for healthy and vigorous growth will already have been laid.

Rotation Contributes to Production

Two forms of natural equalization can be incorporated into an organic gar-

den: crop rotation and mixed plantings. The annual harvesting of specific crops at specific seasons is an idea borrowed from commercial agriculture; the concept of mixed plantings traces its origin back to nature.

In order to establish the three-year crop-rotation plan, gardeners will have to divide their plots into four quarters, each with a number of different beds. The first quarter is reserved for the "hearty eaters," the second for the "normal eaters," the third for "light eaters," and the fourth for stationary plants that do not change their location.

The principle of crop rotation lies in annual alternation: The bed for the current year's hearty eaters will be used for the following year's normal eaters. The beds of this year's normal eaters will still provide next year's light eaters with sufficient nutrients. The bed at the end of the cycle must always be freshly fertilized and enriched with nutrients for the next crop of hearty eaters. In order to maintain the proper sequence, an organic gardener should sketch a simple plan that includes all the vegetable beds. Every year he or she should carefully record the names of the rotated crops in each of these beds.

Hearty Eaters need compost and organic fertilizers such as mixtures of compost and animal manure, dried cow manure or horn-blood-and-bone meal. Stone meal and liquid manures can be added as a supplement. All varieties of cabbages, cucumbers, leeks, celery, and pumpkins rank among the hearty eaters in a vegetable garden. Some people consider potatoes part of this group, others rel-

Crop Rotation and Mixed Planting

egate them to the group of medium appetite.

As a rule, **Normal Eaters** are satisfied with compost. If it seems necessary, the gardener can add small amounts of organic fertilizers or liquid manure made from stinging nettles. The normal eaters include onions, carrots, red beets, kohlrabi, spinach, lettuce, black and red radishes, paprika, and melons.

Light Eaters can survive for a whole year on the leftovers from the more demanding plants. These beds only need tending with compost. Light eaters are peas, beans, and herbs.

The plants that stay in the same place year after year are relegated to the **Fourth Quarter.** They include rhubarb, asparagus, and strawberries. Tomatoes ought to be planted in a sunny section of this quarter, because they are best replanted every year in their own waste of the previous season. They thrive much better without rotation.

Following Nature's Model: Mixed Plantings

The mixed-planting method is a natural form of crop rotation. Under this method, the crops do not vary seasonally from year to year, but vary geographically from row to row in a single bed. A very colorful mixed community of plants thus develops in perfect keeping with nature's model. Like the many different plants growing wild along the side of a country road, the different varieties of vegetables in the garden beds should also be encouraged as much as possible. They take differing amounts of nutrients from the soil, but in return deposit different substances in the soil via their roots.

The above-ground arrangement should be planned so that the leaves and branches of one plant do not interfere with those of another. It is thus a good idea to alternate slender plants with broad and bushy ones. Expansive cabbage heads can be bordered by narrow rows of lettuce plants. Deep-rooting carrots get on very well with flat-growing onions.

With this end in mind, organic gardeners should try to envision the mature size of their spring plantings and choose appropriate neighbors. A further advantage of skillfully arranged mixed plantings is the fact that they form a dense cover in the summer. This is the highy desired shade that keeps the soil friable. Moreover, the moisture in the soil is thus protected for a mulch cover.

Beginning as well as experienced organic gardeners are thus advised always to draw up a carefully designed blueprint for the different vegetables in their mixed plantings. This will be of help in the following years in alternating the main crops in the different beds, and will thus avoid a one-sided exploitation of the soil. The most important consideration for healthy mixed plantings, however, is the decision concerning the positioning of the individual plants. Adjacent rows should be sown only with plants that have a mutually beneficial effect on one another.

The predominant cause of defense reactions or "green animosities" is probably the different fragrances and the root deposits of close neighbors. In any case, one thing is certain: Practical gardening experience repeatedly demonstrates that certain plants

Crop Rotation and Mixed Planting

encourage each other's growth while others are apparently so uncomfortable together that they begin to wilt. Moreover, there are certain combinations that encourage each other in the development of fragrance and taste; these include radishes with cress or potatoes with cumin. Some plants even protect their neighbors from garden pests: The intense odor of tomatoes, for instance, protects cabbages from cabbage butterflies.

Organic gardeners would do well to work their way slowly toward an understanding of the "green relations" in their gardens if they want to translate them to reality. In the beginning, one should resort to the old and true lessons gleaned from experience. Once these have been fully assimilated, one can easily and safely move on to one's own experiments. This interesting field of plant proximity has by no means been exhaustively studied. If you keep your eyes open and are patient enough to try a few experiments of your own, you will surely make many interesting discoveries.

Suggestions

In order to spare the gardener from being inundated with the almost inexhaustible range of possible combinations, the next few pages will describe several arrangements that have already proven viable. Each organic gardener can translate them for himself or herself in keeping with the conditions of their own gardens. You will not have to wait long to reap your reward.

First Bed
Head or leaf lettuce, early kohlrabi, cress, radishes.

This is a classic spring combination that can be planted in alternating rows. Instead of red radishes, you can also grow a tender, early, pinkish-white variety. If you are not a cress fan, you should plan to sow a row of mixed herbs like dill, borage, and chervil next to your row of lettuce.

This spring bed is ready for harvest in a few brief weeks, leaving space for later plantings such as winter leeks alternating with winter carrots. Or late bush beans (June sowing) and late kohlrabi.

Second Bed

Early carrots and onions or late carrots and winter leeks.

This combination is known far beyond the bounds of the organic garden and has been popular among gardeners for generations. These plants mutually defend each other against carrot and onion flies. However, the organic gardener can rely upon this propitious arrangement only if he or she also observes all the other steps necessary for the natural care of the garden.

Third Bed

Bush beans, red beets, savory.

Plant an inside row of bush beans, then a middle row of red beets, followed by another row of green bush beans. The savory should be planted on the outermost edges of the bed and at the head and foot ends. The intensely aromatic savory defends against the black lice that are all too eager to attack tender bean sprouts. Moreover, this arrangement simultaneously produces the ideal seasoning for fresh green beans.

Fourth Bed

Tomatoes, celery, cabbage.

These vigorous vegetables thrive gloriously in close proximity to one another, but they do need a lot of room. They can be fertilized as a group with a dose of stinging-nettle liquid manure, and it is comforting to remember that the tomatoes protect the cabbage from cabbage butterflies. For this mixed planting you can choose among many combinations: Kohlrabi is recommended for small gardens. Larger beds can support broccoli, cauliflower, or savoy cabbage.

Fifth Bed

Cucumbers, dill, peas.

When planted among cucumbers, dill frequently flourishes better than it does in herb gardens. The peas form an effective wind screen, thus providing the cucumbers with their needed warmth, while the long, leafy stems of the pea plants cover the surface of the bed and help retain the moisture.

Sixth Bed

Strawberries, shallots, garlic.

Plant the garlic cloves between the individual strawberry plants and the shallots in a row between the rows of strawberries. Onions as well as garlic help keep the sweet berries healthy, and they protect against fungus diseases. Moreover, they let you use the free spaces in the strawberry patch to plant other things that are not mutually inimical.

These suggestions for possible garden-bed arrangements can simultaneously serve as a brief introduction to some important examples of compatible plant neighbors that either promote the vigorous growth of both or else protect one another against various pests and diseases. Numerous other plants are totally indifferent to one another, and only a few combinations are so unfavorable that one need fear real damage. By keeping these negative combinations in mind, an organic gardener is unlikely to make any horrendous errors as far as the rest of his or her planting plans are concerned.

The same rule holds for organically mixed plantings as for the whole garden: Practice makes perfect. Of course, different climatic and soil conditions play a role in all experiments. Organic gardeners have to discover through their own personal observation which combinations work best under the specific conditions in their gardens.

Bad Neighbors

Beans and peas
Beans and onions
Cabbage and onions
Cabbage and mustard greens
Cabbage and strawberries
Tomatoes and fennel
Tomatoes and potatoes
Tomatoes and peas
Potatoes and sunflowers
Potatoes and celery

Pest Control

In an organic garden there is never a need to eliminate burdensome "dinner guests." The Introduction of this book has already explained that nature knows no such thing as a "pest." Every single creature fulfills a useful function within the broad ramifications of the ecological system. And no gardener may erase these functionaries with impunity.

We therefore have to relearn how to live together with the larger and the smaller creatures of this earth. When they are no longer satisfied with the

Red ladybugs are well known and well liked.

Just as useful: a yellow ladybug.

apples on his tree and begin to eat away the very hairs on his head, however, even the most patient of organic gardeners has to defend himself. He should try to keep insects, slugs, mice, and mildew under reasonable control, but instead of battling these pests head-on, he should consciously choose the path of defense. One of the most important responsibilities of any organic gardener, then, is to become familiar not only with the recipes and various solutions of the natural means of pest control, but also with his allies in the animal and plant world. They can spare him a lot of work, for many useful animals keep insects and caterpillars in check.

A great number of plants drive butterflies with "hostile" intentions, lice, or slugs away from the plantings simply by means of their scent. The following information, although brief, will serve an organic gardener well in his or her everyday activities in the garden.

Animals Can Help

The insects and slugs that make the lives of many gardeners difficult are themselves part of the daily, or nightly, menu of many useful small animals. Wherever they may congregate in an organic garden, considerable numbers of these "pests" soon fall victim to porcupines, toads, frogs, shrews, and moles.

During the summer many different birds carry lice and caterpillars to their sometimes distant nests to feed their young. Even spiders, beetles, and insects participate in the hunt for these thin-skinned plant-eaters. Ladybugs and their larvae, the larvae of

Pest Control

field flies, ichneumon flies, and syrphus flies rank high among the allies of every organic gardener.

Earwigs have by now become one of the trademarks of an organic garden. Even many beginning organic gardeners know that these mobile brown creatures with their rear pincers join the nightly hunt for lice. They spend their daylight hours trying to protect themselves from enemies. An informed organic gardener will thus provide them with a safe and warm refuge in the form of flower pots tightly packed with wood shavings or straw and hung upside down in fruit trees. In this way the earwigs do not even have to leave home to devour black-cherry lice or green-peach leaf lice.

A do-it-yourself earwig nest in a flower pot.

Plants Can Help

Among the unobtrusive plants that never budge from their places can be found a multitude of successful pest-hunters. Smart gardeners take advantage of the natural characteristics of these plants. The protective quality usually resides in their root secretions or in their strong scents.

Savory keeps black lice away, especially from bush beans.

Spice plants with strong fragrances, such as sage, rosemary, thyme, southernwood, and peppermint, ward off cabbage butterflies and slugs. Borders of such aromatic plants, however, are never totally effective. They form a type of barrier at best, but, when combined with other organic measures, they can be a considerable help.

Broom protects young seedlings, especially black and red radishes, cabbages, and cucumbers, from ground fleas. These blooming twigs should be planted very close to the rows of seedlings. This is an old remedy that also helps protect chickens and pigeons against the vermin in their coops.

Savory protects beans from lice.

Preventing lice: nasturtiums and lavender.

Marigolds help guard against nematodes.

The **fritillaria** plant usually keeps voles at a distance simply by means of the intense garlic scent of its bulbs, but it is not a reliable panacea.

The smell of **nasturtiums** has a negative effect on woolly lice, and organic gardeners thus like to spread it on wood chips. These pretty plants can also be used in the battle against aphids. As if by magic, they attract these voracious sucking insects and can thus save many valuable plants from the ravages of such pests.

Garlic has a generally germicidal and fungicidal effect. This is why these bulbs are used as a prophylactic planting against fungus diseases. Organic gardeners plant garlic between strawberries, next to roses, and beneath fruit trees.

Lavender defends against ants to a certain extent and protects roses from aphids. When part of a mixed planting, lavender also has the additional advantage of providing an attractive garden profile.

In many organic gardens **mustard** is used as a defensive plant against snails and slugs, but its effectiveness is disputed. It seems to depend in part upon the condition of the soil, the climate, and upon the degree of concentration of the ethereal mustard oil in the plants.

Marigolds work underground. Their roots contain a nematocidal substance which sterilizes the dangerous root nematodes and thus prevents their reproduction. The infested soil then has time to regenerate itself.

Absinthe is distinguished by its intense, strong odor which tends to ward off vermin. This characteristic has been known and exploited for centuries. Organic gardeners usually plant absinthe, or wormwood as it is also called, near currants. It is said to keep the bushes free from rust.

Onions tend to have a fungicidal effect similar to that of garlic, and are therefore planted between strawberry plants. In the vicinity of carrots they keep carrot flies away.

Homemade Disinfectants

If the numerous animals and carefully selected mixed plantings do their part in keeping the garden free from "pests," very little remains for the organic gardener to do. The ancient reciprocal processes of eating and being eaten result in an ecological balance, and dangerous extremes are thus avoided. Nevertheless, even a peaceable gardener who works in harmony with nature has to know how to deal with emergencies. And such emergency situations can come particularly when he or she first converts to organic methods of gardening. Moreover, extraordinary weather conditions such as a prolonged drought or constant rainfall can bring diseases in their wake. In such instances organic plant disinfectants that have been prepared from natural ingredients grown in the organic garden itself can help. Many of these homemade sprays are particularly effective if they are used as a preventive measure. The important thing is not to let it come to an emergency situation.

Beginning organic gardeners should become thoroughly familiar with the following recipes and learn to recognize the plants that are required for the most important solutions. They can either be found in the natural habitats of stinging nettles, horsetail, fern,

Wild tansy is widespread.

and tansy, or they can be included as wild flowers in one's own garden. Horsetail, of course, which reproduces itself by means of deep runners, should not be voluntarily introduced into a private plot. This siliceous, medicinal herb dates back to time immemorial and is extremely difficult to remove once it has taken hold in a particular location.

The following solutions can be prepared with either fresh or dried herbs.

Pest Control

Absolutely fresh leaves are necessary only for the preparation of the caustic stinging-nettle brew. One can purchase dried herbs in drugstores, health-food centers, herb outlets, and from organic-gardening catalogues. Furthermore, horsetail and stinging-nettle preparations are now commercially available in the usual gardening centers.

Caustic Stinging-Nettle Spray

Fill a 3-gallon bucket with freshly cut stinging nettles. The plants should not yet have set their seeds. Pour water, preferably rainwater, over the nettles until they are completely covered. Let this initial mixture stand for a while, but no longer than 12 to 24 hours. The liquid should not be allowed to ferment! This combination of stinging nettles and cold water should be poured or sprayed undiluted over

A solution of stinging nettles and cold water is used as a spray.

plants that are susceptible to lice infestation. The caustic substance of green nettles is contained only in the freshly made solution. Spray repeatedly every few days. This homemade preparation is most effective against minimal or only slight infestations. In the event of a stronger invasion, even an organic gardener has to take the exceptional step of resorting to the more extreme measures that are described at the end of this chapter.

Field-Horsetail Spray

This is the classical organic prophylactic against fungus diseases. Field horsetail (Equisetum arvense) contains an unusual amount of silicic acid. Organic gardeners can almost feel this crystalline substance between their fingers if they rub the brittle but fragile "blades" in their hands. The silicic acid strengthens the cells of the plants and thus makes them more resistant against the penetration of fungus infections.

For 3 gallons of water you need 2 pounds of fresh or 150 grams of dried horsetail plants without their roots. The herb should soak in water for 24 hours, after which it should be boiled. Let it continue to simmer lightly for approximately 30 minutes. Once the liquid has cooled, it must be run through a sieve.

This horsetail solution should be diluted 1 part solution to 5 parts water (preferably rainwater) and is then ready to be sprayed over the plants susceptible to fungus infestation. Unlike most other sprays, this silicic-acid preparation should be applied in the morning sunshine. The prophylactic effect is increased if this solution is sprayed every 2 to 3 weeks.

Pest Control

Male-fern plants thrive in the garden as well as in the forest.

Male-Fern Solution

To make this solution, the leaves of the male fern *(Dryopteris felix-mas)* are placed in water. You will need about 2 pounds of fresh fern leaves or 100 grams of dried herbs for 3 gallons of water. Male fern is applied either as a brew, like the horsetail solution, or as a fermented liquid manure, like the stinging-nettle solution (see recipe, p. 60). The prepared liquid is sprayed during the winter in undiluted form on trees and woody plants that are plagued with scale insects, slimy insects, and woolly lice.

Tansy Solution

Tansy *(Tanacetum vulgare)* is an aromatic roadside weed with yellow, buttonlike flowers. Mix 300 to 500 grams of fresh tansy (the whole blooming plant) or 30 grams of dried herbs in 3 gallons of water. You can prepare either a brew from this by following the recipe for horsetail solution or a liquid manure by following the recipe for stinging nettles.

This strongly aromatic herb is generally effective in protecting against vermin. It has been used for centuries for this very purpose in the home as well as the garden. The tansy solution should be sprayed on plants in undiluted form during the winter. In the summer this liquid can also be used to water the soil. If you want to spray your fruit-bearing plants after the bloom, you should dilute the solution in the proportion of 1 part liquid to 2 parts water. Tansy sprays help ward off many kinds of "vermin," including primarily strawberry anthonomus, strawberry mites, and blackberry mites.

CAUTION! Tansy contains poisonous substances. Children should be prevented from drinking this solution at all costs.

Absinthe Solution

The sharply bitter wormwood *(Artemisia absinthium)* is similar in effect to tansy because of its strong scent. 300 to 500 grams of freshly picked absinthe or 30 grams of dried herbs suffice for 3 gallons of water. From this you can make a solution (see the horsetail recipe on p. 60), a liquid manure (see the stinging-nettle recipe on p. 60), or a tea. To make the latter, bring the water to a boil and pour it over the leaves. The tea should be covered and allowed to steep for 10 to 15 minutes, after which it can be strained and used when cool. The liquid manure made from absinthe is meant to be sprayed in undiluted concentrations in spring. It wards off aphids, rust on currants, blackberry mites, caterpillars, and ants. Absinthe

Pest Control

tea should be diluted 1 part to 3 with water and sprayed in June and July to ward off aphids and codling moths *(Carpocapsa pomonella)*. In the fall you may want to use 1 part absinthe solution diluted with 2 parts water to protect against blackberry mites.

Tomato-Leaf Extract

Gather some tomato leaves together with their stems and cover them with about 1 gallon of water. The solution should be left to steep for approximately 3 hours. Using a fine spray, sprinkle the liquid from the strong-smelling tomato leaves over young cabbage plants every other day. This will protect the heads from cabbage butterflies, which find this strong odor irritating.

Onion-Peel Solution

20 to 50 grams of onion peels should be covered with about 1 quart of water. Let the solution stand and steep for 4 to 7 days, then filter out the liquid and spray it undiluted over the plants to protect them against mites and fungus diseases.

Soft-Soap Solution

To make this effective and rapidly working prophylactic that has been known and used for generations, you will need to buy pure brown soap in a drugstore or health store. Stir up a mixture of 150–300 grams of soap to about 3 gallons of water. This solution is very reliable against lice, but it should be used only in emergency situations.

Quassia Solution

A solution can be prepared from the tropical quassia wood, which can be purchased in local apothecary shops. You will need 150 grams of quassia and 1 quart of water. In order to increase the effectiveness, you can add to this mixture about 1 quart of horsetail tea and 3 gallons of soft-soap solution. The quassia preparation acts as a caustic organic toxin against aphids and other insects. But, like the commercially available pyrethrum preparations, it also eliminates useful insects. This is why such home-made solutions, even if they are prepared from natural ingredients, should be used only for specific purposes and only in emergency situations.

Commercially Available Organic Preparations

As recently as 10 years ago it was still a difficult and inconvenient task to discover commercial sources of organic plant insecticides. Only a few well-informed gardeners knew where to obtain them. But today a considerable number of organic preparations are offered on the open market. Even the catalogues of mail-order garden centers advertise organic manures and plant insecticides next to their array of chemical products. The largest and most reliable selection of organic insecticides is still available only from certain special firms which are not only in the retail garden business but which also encourage the propagation of organic gardening. These outlets can supply the gardener with necessary tools and equipment as well as provide information concerning other outlets or garden centers in the gardener's more immediate

A selection of commercial preparations for the organic protection and care of plants.

vicinity. The actual choice of product will depend upon its proven reliability and usefulness, and this is important, for the beginner frequently runs into difficulty when it comes to finding his way around the "green market." Some dealers are merely interested in climbing aboard the "organic bandwagon" and thus making a financial gain. After a while even the beginning organic gardener will become familiar with the available products and will know which ones address the particular problems in his or her own garden.

The following section will mention only a few of the many commercial preparations now on the market and will focus on their practical application.

Various pyrethrum products are available for the battle against lice and other insects. These preparations contain a natural poison obtained from the blossoms of African daisies. They are very reliable, the only drawback being that they also affect useful insects. For this reason, organic gardeners should not use these preparations indiscriminately against every single louse. The decision as to when to apply this organic toxin has to be weighed with patience and counterbalanced with a strong sense of responsibility. Dried stinging nettles and various horsetail preparations are also available on the market. The commercial organic preparations against fungus diseases should likewise be used only for preventive purposes.

Also useful for organic gardeners who cannot yet produce their own homemade pesticides are the various preparations made for fruit trees. These products contain, among other things, peat moss, herbal essences, and silicic acid, and they can be obtained from most garden centers or outlets. These light, natural "paints" care for the trunk and branches; they

Pest Control

protect fruit trees and berry bushes from cracks due to frost and from insect pests that bore their way into and under the smooth bark.

A good way to learn more about the various preparations and fertilizers for natural plant care is to collect the catalogues and brochures of the firms directly involved in their production. In addition, every reputable dealer can be expected to be well informed about the products he sells.

How to Deal with "Plague Conditions"

Several diseases and certain kinds of pests are particularly widespread. Every gardener is confronted at one time or another with the problem of defending his garden against them and of keeping them within manageable limits. The following practical tips are meant to be of help in this endeavor.

Downy Mildew

This fungus disease takes on the form of a dusty white coating on leaves and buds. It can attack roses, cucumbers, and fruit trees as well as other plants. In an organic garden this type of mildew, like other fungus diseases, should be treated primarily from a preventive approach.

First of all, a favorable location with a sufficient amount of space between the plants and the organic care of the soil are important prerequisites in

Mildew on cucumbers.

A leaf louse laying eggs on a rosebush.

Pest Control

making plants resistant to such diseases. Moreover, organic gardeners should spray the horsetail solution starting in the spring and continuing into late summer. Mixed plantings of onions and garlic also have a favorable effect. If the dusty white mold is already present, only commercially available fungicides will help.

Plant Lice

Plant lice come in many shapes and colors; they may be green or black; they may be mealy. They damage plants by sucking the nourishment out of their leaves. Most susceptible are the weaker plants. This weakness can be due to too much fertilizer, a lack of necessary nutrients, or even an unfavorable location.

Organic gardeners should thus take the trouble to provide good, natural growing conditions for their plants. In addition, it goes without saying that they should attempt to introduce as many of these pests' natural enemies as possible into the garden. These include, among others, birds, ladybugs, ichneumon flies, syrphus flies, and earwigs.

There is another way to keep the plant-lice invasion under control, however, and this involves measures that also tend to strengthen the plants from within: an application of stinging-nettle manure or a dusting of the leaves with algae preparations or stone meal often helps tremendously.

With an average case you can use the caustic stinging-nettle solution or you may simply want to spray the plants with cold water. In cases of a more serious infestation, quassia or soft-soap solutions or even pyrethrum can be used.

A large rhubarb leaf makes a good slug trap.

Slugs

These voracious animals can cause even the most patient organic gardener a great deal of grief. The unusually large numbers of slugs that have appeared in many gardens in the past few years are a clear indication that the ecological equilibrium has gotten out of balance.

The first remedy an organic gardener should try is to set as many natural enemies as possible on the hunt in the garden, and these include hedgehogs, toads, blindworms, birds, ground beetles, moles, and shrews. Moreover, tansy mulch, tomato-leaf mulch, mustard greens, and nasturtiums tend to ward off slugs, to a certain extent.

Particularly endangered plants can be surrounded by protective barriers made of acrid sand, sawdust, or barley chaff. Stone meal, lime, and wood ashes also act as an obstacle, for these slimy animals find them unpleasant. The problem here is that

A view into a vole nest.

A leek chewed off by voles.

these measures can be applied only in dry weather; they have no effect whatsoever when wet.

Patient organic gardeners can actually catch large numbers of slugs if they set the right traps. These little creatures like to gather under planks of wood, damp sacks, and large leaves because these provide protection against heat and sunlight.

Most effective of these measures are the beer traps. Well-constructed receptacles are commercially available—yogurt cups, for instance, can be buried up to the rim in the ground and filled with beer in the evening. These are very effective traps; the next morning will find the cups filled with slugs of all sizes which met their end in the tempting brew. The cups should be cleaned and refilled on a regular basis. If you apply these various methods consistently, you will begin to see a noticeable improvement as far as the number of slugs in your garden is concerned.

Voles and Field Mice

These small rodents can do a great deal of damage. Their natural enemies, like birds of prey, owls, skunks, and weasels, are rarely found in the vicinity of a private garden, and only the most enterprising of house cats tend to go on a vole hunt.

To eliminate this pest, organic gardeners are best advised to combine as many control measures as possible. Protective plantings of imperial fritillary *(Fritillaria imperialis)*, garlic, euphorbia, and common hound's-tongue *(Cynoglossum officinale)* have a certain prophylactic effect, but they are never completely reliable. Try putting odoriferous substances on the paths, including garlic cloves, fish heads, arborvitae branches, and walnut leaves. Another suggestion is to bury bottles with their necks at an angle because the sound the wind produces as it passes over the opening is very irritating to voles.

The surest, but also unfortunately fatal, means of dealing with these rodents is to use the traps that many garden centers sell as well as the various poisonous baits. The gardener must never touch any of these defensive mechanisms or preparations with bare hands—gloves are absolutely necessary, for, besides protecting

Pest Control

one's hands, gloves also prevent the spreading of a human scent which acts as a warning signal for these animals.

As you can see, even in an organic garden there are numerous means at one's disposal that can be employed against any excessively hungry or insistent pests. Gardeners should never forget, however, that they do not want to declare war against all the inhabitants of their gardens. Every single positive measure that strengthens and encourages life is more important than the negative approaches that may bring in their wake some form of destruction or death. Even a "natural poison" can act as a murderous weapon. Don't be deceived: The louse in question has to die—the catchword "organic" does

not have any comforting overtones for creatures such as these. Only a sense of responsibility and sympathy, however, can keep the organic gardener from setting out on an all too convenient path of rampant destruction. It is important to keep the end goal always in mind, even in difficult situations: Whoever works consistently and steadily in keeping with ecological and biological guidelines will soon find it unnecessary to react angrily to reversals in the balance of nature in his or her garden.

Once the organic gardener has become familiar with the most important fundamentals of organic gardening, he or she is ready to rethink some previously held convictions and to

A traditional kitchen garden usually has a central hub and a symmetrical division of beds.

The Most Important Tasks

apply the gentle green theory in his or her own garden. A new attitude and good intentions can be quickly transformed into practice.

A Garden Plan

Despite all forbearance and patience as far as nature is concerned, gardeners have to keep the big picture in mind when planning a vegetable garden. There has to be a certain degree of organization so that crop rotation and mixed plantings do not interfere with one another. Marigolds along the edges of the beds and sunflowers along the fence will ensure that the vegetable plants can flourish in a cheerful atmosphere.

Organic gardeners should devote the peaceful winter months to devising a simple plan that incorporates all the garden beds. It can be updated every year by simply noting the new or rotating plantings. In this way you can easily keep track of what should be planted where and when. In a new garden the beds and paths can be practically and clearly arranged right from the start. The usual width of a bed that is easy to tend is about 4'. Clearly marked and unobstructed paths should be delineated between the beds, and they usually range between 12" and 19" wide. Remember that you will want to get to the beds with baskets for harvest as well as wheelbarrows full of compost material! The simplest paths are made by stamping the ground with your feet and then covering these trails with boards. Flagstones and concrete slabs are durable and easy to keep clean, but they do have to be set into a sandy foundation.

An essential part of a well-conceived organic-garden plan is, naturally, an easily accessible corner for compost and liquid-manure barrels. The best location is toward the back of the garden behind a screen of bushes or tall sunflowers.

Preparing the Beds

Fall is the best time to prepare the soil for a new and fruitful garden year. If you miss this season, you can always spread new compost and manures early the following spring.

All the beds should be thoroughly weeded and the soil loosened right after the harvest and while the summer blooms are beginning to fade (see the chapter "Spadework? No Thanks!"). One thing to keep in mind while doing this is to make sure that the natural soil layers are not disturbed.

Finally, all free surfaces should be covered with compost. You can use coarse compost in the fall, because it will continue to decompose during the following months. In the spring, particularly right before seeding time, the compost you spread must be ripe and already turned to soil.

The nutrient-containing, homemade humus should be distributed to a depth of about 1½" and then lightly worked into the upper layer of soil with a rake or a hoe. This light contact is enough to establish lively relations between the compost and the garden soil. In addition, you may want to sprinkle a slowly working organic manure wherever you intend to plant rather demanding vegetables or flowers. These sources of nutrients will then be available to the organisms in the soil when they need them in the spring. Manures, too, should be only lightly worked into the soil. The final step is to cover all the open surfaces with a blanket of mulch from leaves, grass, or cut-up weeds.

If you started a new garden toward the end of summer, you will have no compost at your disposal. What you can do, though, is gather all organic waste materials and sow a rapid-growing green manure into all the loosened beds. When the leaves freeze, they provide a good mulch cover for the garden, and by the time spring returns, you will discover loose soil and the beginnings of a humus layer beneath this mulch cover.

Whatever remains of the mulch cover should be removed from all the beds in the spring. The gardener need only comb through the crumbly soil beneath it one more time. The surface of the beds is now ready to be raked smooth and be planted with the first seeds of the new year.

Sowing Under Glass and Plastic

Springtime can mean weeks of cold weather. Seeds, however, need warmth to germinate. This is why resourceful gardeners have always tried to give the weather a boost in hopes of being able to harvest fresh vitamins early in the year. A protective covering over seedlings and young-plant beds can produce a moist and warm atmosphere that is very conducive to the early growth of green plants.

The good old hotbed is still the best candidate for this purpose. Handy gardeners can build their own, for it con-

Peat and plastic pots for indoor germination.

A mini-greenhouse for flowers and tomatoes.

sists of nothing more than a wooden box with windows on top. The back wall should be a bit higher than the front one, so that the cover slopes on an angle. Glass windows are heavy and can be broken easily. Lighter and more practical are Plexiglas panes or a wooden frame that is covered with a sheet of plastic food-wrap. If you are not a do-it-yourselfer, you can buy well-constructed hotbeds in many garden centers.

The Most Important Tasks

These boxes should be turned toward the south so that the gardener can capitalize as much as possible on the warmth of the sun. The windows must be able to be opened for ventilation. A simple stick is frequently all that is needed to hold them up.

An additional source of ground heating can be built into the hotbed if the gardener digs out about 15″–24″ of dirt and fills the hole in February, when the weather is clear, with about 7″–12″ of fresh horse manure. This manure, which produces heat rapidly, should be stamped down and covered with about 7″ or so of good garden humus. This type of manuring warms the ground and thus provides the ideal conditions for seed germination.

Easily available and very convenient are the modern foil tunnels. Here, too, organic gardeners have a choice between doing it themselves or buying the finished product. A few round arches made from stiff wire or iron are simply placed in the ground and covered with a plastic sheet. Boards and stones should be placed on the part of the sheet that rests on the ground to prevent it from being blown away. Under this protective roof of plastic you can start planting as early as the end of February or the beginning of March. Lettuce, radishes, kohlrabi, and the first herbs thrive well under such conditions. They grow rapidly in this humid greenhouse atmosphere and provide the first green harvest after many long winter months. Naturally, you can also raise some summer flowers and vegetables that need a lot of warmth in this kind of protective bed.

If you are the fortunate owner of your own small greenhouse, you can set preliminary cultures of your plants under particularly favorable conditions. But there is even a simpler way: Establish a nursery on your windowsill. As early as March, paprika, tomatoes, timothy, basil, and other plants that otherwise have to be protected from the cold at least until May can be seeded in bowls, small boxes, and jars.

Organic gardeners should check early seedlings regularly. When dangerously high temperatures quickly develop under glass or plastic enclosures, tender shoots can be damaged. On sunny days, hotbeds and foil tunnels should be well ventilated, with vents closed again in the early afternoon so that the day's warmth is retained during the night.

Be careful to keep the plants and seedlings "under cover" moist at all

Planting pole beans.

times. The best time to water them is early morning, because it is best to keep the leaves free of moisture during the heat of the day. Not attending to this can easily result in burns and other heat damage to the plant. Watering toward evening is again dangerous, because damp vegetation is prone to putrefaction during cool nights.

Sowing in Open Beds

In clement regions organic gardeners can set their first open seedlings as early as March. In harsher climates they are advised to wait awhile until the ground is once again frost-free and slightly warmed by the sun. Spinach, carrots, and parsley are not sensitive to the cold. A little later come the peas, broad beans, and onions.

There is one important rule of thumb, however: Heavy, loamy soils should be worked before planting, and particularly if they are dry. Wet earth can become clumped and compressed with every step. Impatience in the springtime destroys more than it gains. Winter moisture evaporates more quickly from light, sandy soils; these gardens can often be worked earlier than the others.

No seeds will germinate without a minimal amount of warmth. It is therefore better to wait for a few sunny spring days, for plants that are set a little later in warm weather grow more vigorously and more evenly than those that are set much earlier.

In sowing and planting, keep to the bed arrangement previously described. It is also important to maintain proper spaces between the various plants. Although the seed packages usually indicate the best

A spring bed with a string to ensure straight rows.

time to plant and the distances that should be maintained, the following pages will also provide some important information.

Organic gardeners can keep their rows straight by stretching a piece of twine between two end poles. The rake handle is useful in drawing grooves or furrows for the seeds. These furrows should be filled with finely sifted, ripe compost. The seeds should not be placed too close to one another, because the plants that eventually develop from them will need a lot of air. If they are too close, they get in one another's way. Finally, the back of the rake can be used to carefully cover the newly planted rows of seeds, and they should be watered with a gentle spray. From now on they should be kept uniformly moist. Many a failure in this initial sowing stage is due quite simply to forgetfulness and

The Most Important Tasks

if the germinating seeds dry up, all the work was in vain.

Plant Care

In April and May the seedlings the gardener has purchased as well as those he has raised himself should be transplanted into the ground. In the case of home-grown plants it is essential to isolate them in individual small pots after germination so that they have a chance to develop healthy root systems.

Vigorous vegetables like cabbage, potatoes, lettuce, and leeks can be planted in the open as early as April. Southerners, like tomatoes, paprika, and cucumbers, should be transplanted to open beds only toward the end of May.

Organic gardeners can give their plants a very good head start if they fill the furrows with ripe compost. Stone meal also improves the soil in which

A healthy young plant is set in the earth.

the young plants are to thrive. If you water them with heavily diluted liquid nettle manure, you will likewise improve the conditions for healthy growth.

Seedling holes can be dug in the ground by using a round planting peg. If the soil is soft and friable, your hand is by far the better and more responsive garden tool. Gardeners can use their fingers to feel whether the roots have enough room or the soil is properly packed down. Water generously so that the young plants don't droop. During the next few weeks organic gardeners should perform the most important gardening tasks as regularly as possible: water with warm water, spread the mulch covers, tie up long branches, and remove diseased or withered leaves. If you make a daily tour of your garden, you will have little to do; if you tend to procrastinate and put these tasks off, you will find that only a few weeks later you will have to hack your way through a green wilderness. During May and June the desired plants as well as weeds grow extraordinarily well. It is during this time that the organic gardener has to watch that his garden does not get out of hand.

Harvesting and Preserving

Spring and summer are only a few months long, and the remaining months of the year can be expected to be mostly wet, cold, and gray. Your garden will produce very few fresh vegetables and probably no fruit at all from November to March. Gardeners thus have to prepare for these long, lean weeks; many have found that it pays to carefully put up the nutritious products of their own organic harvests. There are many ways of doing this. One modern and highly recommended method is to freeze them. Many kinds of vegetables and fruit can be preserved extremely well by freezing. Most important of all, though, is the fact that this method retains the vitamins inherent in your produce.

Boiling down, however, also has its advantages, and many kinds of fruit taste better out of a jar than out of the refrigerator. Indispensable, of course, are all the homemade marmalades and jams. They can be kept for a long time in vacuum-sealed glass jars, and in many cases the toilsome sterilization process is superfluous.

Root vegetables can be stored either in a hotbed nursery or in the cellar. The hotbed box intended for this purpose has to be protected against the cold. Straw mats over the windows and a thick layer of leaves against the outer walls help retain

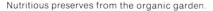

Drying herbs and onions.

heat. Since most modern cellars are too dry and too warm, carrots, celery, red beets, and horseradish roots should be buried in chests in damp sand or peat.

Nutritious preserves from the organic garden.

Lettuce Is Indispensable

Today's organic gardeners are not the first to tie cabbage heads together by their stalks and hang them upside down from the ceiling; others include carefully spreading out apples and pears on ventilated wooden grates. Onions and garlic, too, need a dry storage place.

Worth remembering also: putting foodstuffs up in stoneware pots and crocks. These receptacles turn white cabbage into sauerkraut, and beans can be preserved with salt. Pickles, red beets, and pumpkins maintain their freshness for a long time in a spicy vinegar solution. Herbs, beans, apples, pears, and plums can also last the winter if they are properly dried.

Whoever is interested can find recipes and more detailed instructions concerning the various methods of preserving fruits and vegetables in books that deal specifically with these topics. There is one important principle, however, that is applicable for all types of food storage: Only unblemished, healthy fruits and vegetables can be preserved over a period of time. This is why harvesting has to be done extremely carefully. Use care in pulling your carrots and red beets out of the ground, and make sure the apples do not fall to the ground and develop brown spots. These efforts will pay off, for the gardener and his or her family can live for a long time on the fruits of their labors. During the winter months these nutritious foodstuffs help considerably in maintaining resistance against common colds and other ailments.

The gardening year begins in the spring with your first tender head of

Red and green varieties of leaf lettuce.

lettuce and ends in the winter with the firm lamb's-lettuce *(Valerianella olitoria)*. Skilled gardeners who value healthy, vitamin-rich food and are lucky enough to live in temperate climes can ensure 12 uninterrupted months of ever different varieties of lettuce harvests. It all depends upon proper and timely planting, and it certainly does not require any esoteric knowledge or extraordinary skills. Even a beginner finds it easy to raise large quantities of this undemanding "companion" in his or her garden.

All lettuces flourish well as a second crop, for they do not need strong fertilizers and do not even need their own bed. A few heads of summer lettuce or endive can be planted wherever there is enough space for them. Leaf lettuce is quite content along the edge of a bed, where it forms an attractive as well as practical border. **Head Lettuce** thrives best in a sunny location. You should plant it in rows

Lettuce Is Indispensable

Young sugar-loaf lettuce.

Iceberg lettuce forms thick, crispy heads.

about 9" apart. The spring varieties are as tender as butter and can be planted in March and April. From April to May the summer lettuces are ready to be planted. They have firmer leaves and do not sprout as quickly in the heat. Autumn is the time to plant winter lettuce and it will be the first to ripen in the coming spring.

Fertilizer: Compost and liquid sting-ing-nettle manure.

Protection: The young plants should be protected against slugs (see p. 65).

Mixed Plantings: Radishes, kohlrabi, strawberries, cabbage, tomatoes, onions, beans.

Leaf Lettuce is particularly recommended for small gardens. It does not grow in heads and can be planted in rows. The leaves can be picked or cut repeatedly. The harvest period lasts for weeks, sometimes even months. Sow small amounts at any one time, leaving sufficient space between plants. This practical and lasting lettuce bridges over every hiatus in the

harvesting of other varieties of lettuce. In addition, there are green, reddish-brown, and red-leafed varieties.

Fertilizer: Compost and liquid sting-ing-nettle solution.

Protection: Young plants and seedlings should be protected against slugs (see p. 65).

Mixed Plantings: Tomatoes, red and black radishes, comfrey, red beets, asparagus, fennel, and cabbage.

Iceberg Lettuce is a crispy summer lettuce that grows in the form of heads. It can tolerate a great deal of heat and remains fresh for a long time in the refrigerator.

Fertilizer: More liquid stinging-nettle manure than for head lettuce, applied regularly.

Protection: See section on Head Lettuce.

Mixed Plantings: See section on Head Lettuce.

Witloof or French Endive is a member of the chicory family and sets a typical, long taproot. It can be planted in

Vegetables for the Beginning Gardener

its permanent place in the garden in June and then be thinned out at a later time. Witloof forms pointed heads and ripens only in late autumn. This tart winter lettuce can even tolerate several degrees of frost.

Fertilizer: Compost, organic liquid manures, and a little organic fertilizer.
Protection: Should be protected against voles and small rodents.
Mixed Plantings: Fennel.

Radicchio or **Red Chicory** is a winter-hardy lettuce that should be planted from mid-May to mid-June. The long green leaves should be removed in the fall, for only then does the reddish-brown rosette develop. This aromatic lettuce can be harvested from the winter garden from December to spring.

Fertilizer: Compost, organic liquid manures, if necessary a little organic fertilizer.
Protection: Against voles and small rodents.
Mixed Plantings: Winter cabbage.

Endives are one of the most popular of all late lettuces. The summer varieties ripen during the weeks of Indian summer, whereas the curly winter endives can be harvested from autumn to the beginning of winter. They should thus be planted in June. To blanch them, the heads can be tied together, but only in dry weather, for otherwise they tend to rot.

Fertilizer: Compost, stone meal, organic liquid manures.
Protection: These plants should be covered with plastic sheets as a protection against frost.
Mixed Plantings: Cabbage, leeks, fennel.

Lamb's-Lettuce is an important winter lettuce—and just happens to be the variety richest in vitamins. It can be planted in any open bed from August to September. By leaving about 4" between the rows, the gardener will have an easier time of weeding and mulching. There are broad-leafed varieties as well as small-leafed rosettes.

Fertilizer: Compost
Protection: There are no problems because of the lateness of the season.
Mixed Plantings: Winter onions.

The greater the variety of vegetables in a garden, the more successful the mixed plantings and, as a result, the more nutritious the crop for the gardener and his or her family. Nevertheless, beginning organic gardeners should not try everything at once. Only after they have become acquainted with the most important vegetables and their characteristics will they be able to try new experiments from year to year. It is always good to have a slowly acquired but fundamental stock of experience to which one can repeatedly refer. All sorts of excursions into the realm of exotic delicatessen can be undertaken later on. The following pages will present only a cross-section of the great varieties of vegetables that can be grown in organic gardens. During these early stages you should not only heed the directions on the seed packages but should also carefully observe the growth and blooming patterns in your own garden. In this living classroom you can learn more about the laws governing biology than anywhere else—not surprising, since the word "biology" itself means "the study of life."

Spinach is a nutritious, leafy vegetable particularly rich in vitamins and iron. It thrives well in moist soils with high humus content. Moreover, the luxuriant green leaves can be used as a living mulch between other plants. Spinach should be set in the spring between March and May and again in the late summer from August until the end of September. The later seedlings are winter-hardy and can be harvested in the springtime. Spinach should always be picked fresh and young, and this is why a frequent reseeding is necessary. It is also a very good way to fill in empty spots in your garden.

Fertilizer: Compost and stone meal, a little organic fertilizer, such as horn-blood-and-bone meal. Be careful not to add too much nitrogen!

Protection: This plant is not particularly endangered.

Mixed Plantings: Cabbage, tomatoes, pole beans, strawberries, red beets.

Beetroot is another leafy vegetable. There are two main varieties, the common beet and Swiss chard, both of which can be prepared like spinach. Both varieties should be sown in April directly into open beds with about 12"–15" between the individual plants. Later seeding is possible right up to July, and these are even winter-hardy if they are protected with a covering of leaves. Beetroot can be harvested over a long period of time. If the "heart" of the plant remains intact, the leaves will continue to grow.

Fertilizer: Compost and some organic fertilizers.

Protection: Porous sand prevents mildew; this plant should not be densely mulched due to danger of putrefaction.

Mixed Plantings: Carrots, cabbage, radishes.

A rich harvest of wax beans from the mixed planting.

Peas are members of the papilionaceous family of plants. Like so many of the useful green manures, these plants develop nitrogen nodules on their roots. Since they already possess their own "fertilizer factory," peas make very few demands on the gardener. Moreover, they are not sensitive to cold. Those varieties of peas that grow tall need a support structure made of wire mesh or brushwood Peas, the smooth, round fruits of this plant, turn mealy with time. They can be planted as early as March.

Sugar peas are sweet and tender as long as they are young, but they have to be harvested while the pods are still soft and the peas themselves still small. Furthermore, they are best cooked in their pods. These varieties can be sown in April, and should be planted about 2" deep in rows about 15" apart.

Fertilizer: Compost, stone meal, perhaps even wood ashes, but never nitrogen!

Protection: An open, sunny location protects against diseases in the plant. Fertilizers that contain nitrogen have

Vegetables . . .

a negative effect on the natural resistance of peas. In emergency situations, pyrethrum preparations can be used against vetches that bore their way into the pods.

Mixed Plantings: Cucumbers, carrots, lettuce, cabbage, fennel.

Like the peas, **Beans,** too, belong to the family of papilionaceous plants as well as to that of the legumes. There are many different varieties of beans that can adapt to gardens of any size and to any climate. Bean plants make no claims as far as soil and nutrients are concerned, but most varieties need more warmth than peas do.

There are green and yellow varieties of *bush (snap) beans*. They should be planted in May and June. The fat seeds should be sown only about ⅔" deep. The rows should be planted about 15" apart. Bush beans can be picked fresh when needed and make very good vegetables, salads, and soups. They can be boiled, frozen, dried, or salted.

Pole beans are a bit more demanding, for above all else they require tall climbing poles firmly anchored in the ground. The seeds should be planted in a circle around these poles. Make sure that your pole beans are always sufficiently moist during their growing period, but be careful: Raw beans are poisonous! Take precautions to see that children do not pick the pods. The toxic substance phasine is rendered harmless by boiling, after which the beans are nutritious and tasty.

Kidney beans are the most undemanding members of the whole family. They thrive without difficulty even in rugged environments. These high-climbing beans can be planted along fences, where they then serve in the

Red and yellow onions.

additional capacity of a privacy screen. They bear attractive fiery-red and sometimes even white blossoms and produce long and vigorous pods.

Kidney beans have to be picked while young before they become hard and "woolly." The seeds can be dried for winter reserves as well as for new seedlings.

Broad beans are likewise hardy fellows that can be planted in open beds as early as March—the earlier, the better. The rows need about 15" of open space between them, and there should be about 9" to 10" between the individual plants. Let the thick seeds swell up in water before being planted. Broad beans can thrive even in heavy, loamy soils. Their roots penetrate deep into the ground and help to loosen the soil.

Fertilizer: No nitrogen! Bush and broad beans need nothing more than compost. Pole and kidney beans can tolerate a bit of organic fertilizer (without nitrogen).

Protection: Savory protects bush beans against lice; sawdust can be spread around young beans to form a protective barrier against slugs. Broad beans are susceptible to black lice; early sowing and a well-ventilated, roomy location protect against a heavy infestation. Pinch off and destroy the tips that are particularly covered with lice. Mosaic viruses cannot be treated directly; this disease is transmitted by leaf lice, and the only thing you can do here is make sure you have healthy seeds and try to keep the lice under control.

Mixed Plantings: Tomatoes, cucumbers, cabbage, celery, red beets for bush beans; tomatoes, cucumbers, nasturtiums, cabbage for pole beans; lettuce and kohlrabi for broad beans.

Onions are one of the most nutritious of all vegetables. They are a food, a medicine, and a spice all rolled into one. They are also among the least demanding plants in the garden and can flourish as a second crop. Fresh, nitrogen-containing fertilizers harm onions and have a negative effect on their keeping quality.

Yellow and red onions can be sown from seed starting in mid-May. The rows should be at least 8" apart. The young onion plants should be transplanted at a later date with about 2" to 4" between them. Tender white scallions should be planted in August, and they need only 1" between individual plants.

Bulbs and shallots should be planted in April. They need about 8" to 10" between the rows and 4" between the individual plants. Large, single onions grow from bulbs; shallots form a cluster with many small to medium-sized cloves.

All varieties of onions love a sunny bed and loose earth with good drainage. They are ripe when the tubelike

This is how a healthy leek should look.

leaves turn yellow and droop. You should harvest onions when the sun is shining and store them in a dry and well-ventilated place.

Fertilizer: Compost and, in keeping with the condition of the soil, some potash-containing wood ashes; no nitrogen!

Protection: A mixed planting with carrots protects against onion flies.

Mixed Plantings: Carrots, chicory, head lettuce, cucumbers, strawberries, dill, savory.

Leeks are an aromatic winter vegetable that should be a part of every garden. They are related to onions, but make more demands as far as nutrients are concerned. Two seedings are recommended: one from March to April in a hotbed and one from May to June in an open bed. The early plants can be harvested in late summer, while the later planting provides some very welcome winter vegetables. Place the slender leek plants about 6" apart in deep furrows. There should be about 8" to 12" between the rows. The furrows themselves should be raked during the course of the

Vegetables . . .

Carrots grow straight in loose humus.

Red beets are especially nutritious.

summer and the soil heaped up around the individual plants, for this helps produce beautiful white shafts. Make sure these plants are always sufficiently watered.

Fertilizer: Compost and organic fertilizers such as cow or pig manure. Fertilize repeatedly during the growing season with a liquid stinging-nettle manure.

Protection: The leek moth, which bores small channels into the plants, can be discouraged by spreading stone meal and by spraying with horsetail solutions. Diseased plants have to be cut back radically, but don't worry, they will soon develop healthy new shoots.

Mixed Plantings: Carrots, celery, tomatoes, lettuce, cabbage, strawberries.

Celery ranks among the nutritious root vegetables. It needs a moist soil rich in nutrients. These plants can be forced only in warm hotbeds or greenhouses. It is much simpler to buy the seedlings at a gardening center. Celery should not be planted before the middle of May. It should be set very flat and allowed to "wobble" a bit in the beginning. The individual plants need about 15″ of open space in all directions.

Celery should be harvested only late in the fall. The stalks, rich in vitamins and minerals, can be stored in the cellar or a hotbed nursery during the winter months.

Fertilizer: Compost and dung or hornblood-and-bone meal; wood ashes or dried cow manure; stone meal and limestone. If your garden has a salty, coastal soil, sprinkle the celery roots with water that contains dissolved table salt.

Protection: Field-horsetail sprays have a prophylactic effect against fungus diseases such as celery rust.

Mixed Plantings: Leeks, bush beans, cauliflower, tomatoes.

Savoy needs a lot of room and generous fertilizing.

Carrots need deep, loosened soil that must never be fertilized with fresh manure. The seeds of carrot plants can be sown as early as March in open beds. Late winter carrots should be planted in the period between the end of May and the end of June.

Since carrots take a long time to germinate, you should smuggle in a few radish plants to mark the rows. The furrows should be 1" deep and 8" apart. Later the plants that are growing too close to one another ought to be thinned out, and the entire planting should be kept uniformly moist. Carrots that are not eaten right away can be stored in the cellar or in hotbed nurseries toward the end of fall.
Fertilizer: Compost and some liquid stinging-nettle manure in the summer.
Protection: A mixed planting of leeks and onions protects against carrot flies. Also effective against this particular pest are an open, somewhat windy location and sufficient distance between the plants. If you plant early in March and again late in June, you can avoid the seasonal flight of these garden pests.
Mixed Plantings: Onions, leeks, peas, tomatoes, chicory, leaf lettuce, radishes, common beets.

(Red) Beets are as nutritious as they are undemanding. They can thrive even in partial shade. Starting in April, you should plant 2 seeds at a time 4" apart in rows 10" apart. Plants that are too close together can be thinned out later on.

When harvesting red beets, one must be careful not to damage the bulbs, for this will cause the precious sap to run out. Like celery and carrots, vitamin-rich red beets can be stored in nurseries or be put up in sweet-and-sour sauces in stoneware jugs.
Fertilizer: Compost and a little organic liquid manure with comfrey in the summer.
Protection: No particular problems here.
Mixed Plantings: Bush beans, kohlrabi, leaf lettuce, cucumbers, peas.

Cabbage is one of a robust vegetable family encompassing many different members: Red cabbage, white cabbage, savoy, kale, cauliflower, Brussels sprouts, broccoli, and the tender kohlrabi are all related. Like lettuce, kohlrabi can be planted just about anywhere in the garden. It makes no particular claims as far as soil or location is concerned.

The larger varieties of cabbage, on the other hand, are very demanding when it comes to nutrients. In return, though, they provide the gardener with many vitamins and a rich supply of precious mineral salts. All types of

Vegetables . . .

cabbage can be easily planted in hotbeds or in open beds: early varieties like cauliflower in March, late varieties like Brussels sprouts, white and red cabbage, and savoy in April. Set the plants as deep as possible with about 20″ of free space all around. Only the late varieties can be stored for winter use. Broccoli should be seeded with the late varieties and transplanted into beds at the end of May or beginning of June. The green "flowers" can be harvested for months because the plant continually sets tender new sprouts. Kale is the least demanding member of the family. It should be seeded in May or June and planted in already harvested beds from June to August.

Chinese cabbage is a short-lived plant with very rapid growth. It should be sown no earlier than July. This tender cabbage can tolerate a few degrees of frost. Kale and Brussels

sprouts are completely winter-hardy; in fact, they do not taste good until after the first real frost.

Although the large-headed cabbages are very nutritious, the more modest members of the cabbage family, such as kohlrabi, broccoli, kale, and Chinese cabbage save space in garden.

Fertilizer: Compost, stone meal, and generous amounts of organic fertilizer like decomposed dung, dried cow manure, or horn-blood-and-bone meal. During the growing season these plants should be watered repeatedly with liquid stinging-nettle manures. Cabbage needs nitrogen for its expansive leaves, but, as with all fertilizers, you should not overdose plants with organic manures.

Protection: Lime or dolomite limestone sprinkled into the plant pit protects against clubroot. A mixed planting consisting of tomatoes and celery diverts cabbage butterflies. If there is only a slight infestation, the organic gardener should remove the caterpillars regularly by hand and crush the eggs. In the case of a heavy infestation, a pyrethrum preparation, such as *Bacillus thuringiensis,* is neccesary to ward off the butterfly larvae. A soft-soap solution wards off cabbage flies, and stone meal and wood ashes sprinkled over the leaves help keep away lice.

Mixed Plantings: Potatoes, tomatoes, celery, spinach, lettuce, leeks, peas.

Cucumbers should be planted in open beds no earlier than the third week in May, but you can cultivate cucumber plants very early in the year in pots on windowsills or in hotbeds. When planting them outside, set the large seed pods in a slight mound of

Cucumbers.

Tomato blossoms in the leaf axil.

Cherry tomatoes are particularly delicious.

earth 8"—12" high in the middle of the bed. The plants will later need to be spaced about 12" apart because they produce long runners.

Cucumbers need a sunny, protected bed, a soil rich in nutrients, and a great deal of moisture. You might want to train the runners to climb a latticed grid.

When selecting your seeds, you must decide between long, slender salad cucumbers and the short, pickling varieties. These vegetables can be harvested over a period of weeks, and they can be put up for the winter in the form of sweet-and-sour pickles or salted, garlic ones.

Fertilizer: Compost and organic fertilizers; decomposed horse manure is also very good. In the summer, cucumbers should be repeatedly sprayed with organic liquid manures.

Protection: Cucumbers are susceptible to mildew; you should therefore choose mildew-resistant varieties and spray them with horsetail solution as a preventive measure.

Mixed Plantings: Peas, beans, celery, onions, corn, red beets, lettuce, cabbage, fennel, dill, caraway, coriander.

Tomatoes resemble cucumbers in that they, too, are a tropical vegetable —they are indigenous to Central America but have long since become naturalized in other parts of the world. It pays to raise them in even the smallest garden, because individual tomato plants can be easily cultivated in large pots or pails. The red fruits are rich in vitamin C, in minerals, and in natural fruit acids.

Tomatoes are essentially loners. They do not like to be rotated, but rather prefer to remain in the same location year after year. These red "Apples of Paradise," as they are sometimes called, flourish best in their own waste. To date, there is no scientific explanation as to why this is so; all one can say is that experience has proven it to be true.

Tomato seeds germinate quickly and easily. Even a beginning organic gardener can thus cultivate his or her plants without difficulty on a windowsill or in a small greenhouse. A large selection of different varieties is available in seed form from just about all garden centers, whereas the actual tomato plants one might purchase in May usually produce only round fruit or slicing tomatoes.

It is worth the trouble to experiment with the varying cultures to determine one's favorite variety: Round fruits with red or yellow skins; thick, irregu-

Vegetables . . .

larly shaped, meaty slicing tomatoes; bush tomatoes that do not need to be tied; oval plum tomatoes; small, sweet, espaliered types—all are there for the choosing.

All varieties of tomatoes need a very sunny, protected location so that the aromatic fruits can ripen to their fullest. Ideal growing conditions are found in front of a white reflecting wall. These vigorously growing plants are some of the biggest eaters and drinkers in the garden, and thus need a hearty and sufficient supply of nutrients. Plant the young tomatoes as deep as possible, burying them in the ground as far up as the first leaves. This will encourage them to form lateral roots which contribute to the nourishment of these elegant plants. Each individual plant needs a pole to which it can be tied securely. You should allow only two shoots, or three at the most, to grow; all the others should be broken off. The sucker shoots, too, which continuously form in the leaf axils, should be removed

Organically grown potatoes can be recognized by their aroma.

throughout the course of the summer. In late summer, usually toward the end of August, you should also break off the uppermost blossoms and buds so that the plants can direct all their strength to the ripening fruits. On hot days, tomatoes have to be thoroughly and generously watered. Pour water directly over the root area. All tomato debris, including sucker shoots and wilted leaves, should be placed around the plants as a mulch cover. In more rugged areas, tomatoes need a warming plastic hood in the fall so that the remaining fruits can ripen. The last green tomatoes can be hung on their branches in the house until they turn red.

Fertilizer: Compost, stone meal, and ample organic fertilizer such as decayed dung, dried cow manure, horn-blood-and-bone meal, dolomitic limestone, or guano. During the summer months the plants should be watered frequently with liquid stinging-nettle manure and mulched with their own waste.

Protection: You can spray tomato plants with a horsetail solution as a preventive measure against fungus diseases such as brown rot and leaf mold. Particularly suited for tomato plants is a solution consisting of 1 pint of skim milk and 2 quarts of water. The plants should be sprayed with this mixture once every week.

Mixed Plantings: Celery, parsley, lettuce, cabbage, nasturtiums.

Potatoes, like tomatoes, belong to the family of the *Solanaceae.* They came originally from South America. These nutritious apples of the earth, as the Indians called them, are rich in various vitamins, mineral salts, and protein. Their cultivation pays off,

Vegetables . . .

even if there are only two rows of early potatoes. The yellow tubers from the garden taste much better than store-bought white potatoes, which frequently contain a lot of water but little agreeable taste. Potatoes like a loose humus soil rich in nutrients. Seeds from an organically grown culture result in better harvests than those normally offered in commercial establishments.

Germinate the seed pods in a moderately warm room. Once they have sprouted, they can be placed individually in small pots in such a way that the end with the most eyes is facing upward. As soon as the soil reached a temperature of at least 45° F., you can begin to plant. In mild regions this can be as early as the end of March; in more rugged locations the gardener is advised to wait until well into April. It is smarter to plant a little later in good weather than too early in bad. Wetness and cold can result in a shock to the tubers from which they only slowly recover.

Draw the potato furrows 2" deep and about 15"–19" apart. At least 12" should be left between the individual plants in each row. As soon as the foliage begins to grow vigorously, the soil of the potato rows should be heaped up once or twice. In choosing a particular variety, the gardener must decide between early, middle, and late potatoes. The distinction between

mealy and firm varieties also plays a role. When harvesting potatoes, the individual tubers should not be left lying in the sunlight for long, for if they are, they turn green and produce a toxin called solanine. Green spots must be dug out deeply and removed completely.

Early potato varieties should be harvested when the leaves turn brown. This usually happens between June and July, depending upon when they were planted. Later varieties ripen between August and September. These vegetables are best stored in humid cellar rooms, where the temperature must always remain above the freezing point.

Fertilizer: Compost, stone meal, decayed dung, or horn-blood-and-bone meal; in summer an organic liquid manure.

Protection: Spraying with horsetail tea is a preventive measure against fungus diseases such as tuber rot. You can also use commercially available preparations which increase the plants' resistance to fungus infestation. Dust the leaves with lime to protect against potato bugs; collect the bugs and treat them with pyrethrum preparations only as a last resort.

Mixed Plantings: Cabbage, horseradish, peas, broad beans, nasturtiums; caraway improves the aroma of the potato tubers.

The Herb Garden

Arrangement and Care

Herbs can grow in a motley collection in one single bed. The gardener has only to see to it that the tall plants, such as the mighty lovage, are positioned in the back; the medium-sized herbs should be arranged in the middle, and the low ones, like thyme and stonecrop, should grow along the front edge of the bed.

If the herb garden is divided into individual beds that are bordered by stone or wooden slabs, flagstones, or wood shavings, it is easy to oversee and very practical. In this way each herb can flourish on its own and can be easily tended and harvested.

Even if you have only a small space left in your garden, you do not have to renounce these aromatic plants. Herbs can thrive very well on the edge of vegetable beds. They can even find a place in a flower garden, for many herbs bedeck themselves in summer with pretty blossoms. The silvery-gray sage, blue blooming lavender, common rue with its ornamenental foliage, hyssop with its pink and blue flower panicles, and the delicately pinnate southernwood are all small jewels.

Many of the herbs that provide continuous sources of fresh spices for the kitchen can thrive even in small bowls on the terrace, in balcony planters.

However, organic gardeners should become acquainted with a few fundamental rules regarding the healthy growth of these particular plants.

An herb garden needs direct sunlight. Pictured here are valerian, agrimony, red orach, peppermint, and nasturtiums.

The Herb Garden

Most of the herbs that have been growing in our gardens for centuries came originally from warm lands. Most herbs need a lot of sun and a light, rather dry soil with good drainage. Moreover, it is worth remembering that modest conditions are more favorable than luxurious fare for spice plants. Our organic gardener must therefore resist the temptation to feed his or her herbs too well. Nitrogen is particularly intolerable to these plants. When richly fertilized, they do indeed produce luxuriant foliage, but what they gain in appearance they loose in aroma. Medicinal properties and a spicy aroma can develop only as a result of a balanced diet. Good, ripe compost is therefore the best foundation for an herb garden. Additional fertilization is not necessary.

Only a few native herbs form exceptions to this general rule. Chives, sour dock, peppermint, chervil, scurvy grass, and lovage prefer a somewhat moist humus soil. They also flourish in light, partial shade. Tarragon and the vigorous borages can tolerate a somewhat richer diet, but a little of the more slowly working organic manures such as horn shavings suffices for these plants.

If you intend to plant an herb garden in heavy soil, you must first provide a good drainage system and a thorough loosening of the soil. The best way to do this is to mix a generous amount of sand with the loamy humus. If the substratum of the garden is nonporous, a good suggestion is to plant herbs in an elevated bed. Hints concerning the harvesting and the best methods of conserving these various herbs are included in the brief descriptions that follow.

Annual Herbs

Most annual herbs can be planted in open beds directly from their seed packages. The best time is spring—that is, from April to May. Only a few varieties are particularly sensitive to the cold, and these the organic gardener should cultivate on a sunny windowsill or in hotbeds.

Basil is a wonderful spice that came originally from the sunny south. It is easy to grow when the seeds are left to germinate in pots or bowls on a warm windowsill. By mid-May these seedlings will be ready for transplanting into open beds. Experienced herb gardeners always keep a few basil seedlings in a flower pot, for if the summer turns out to be cold and rainy, these pots can be returned to a bright and warm windowsill. They will thrive better there than will the basil planted in the now hostile open beds. In the garden this herb needs a protected location, compost, and a soil rich in humus. The individual plants need about 8″ to 10″ of empty space between them.

Spice and Medicinal Properties: Basil has a sweet and pungent taste, slightly hot and peppery. This kitchen spice has an unusual and noble fragrance. The essential oil in the leaves has a soothing effect on the stomach, intestines, and nerves.

Harvest and Use: The young leaves can be picked fresh as needed throughout the summer. This herb, however, does lose all its aroma when used in any preserved food. Basil improves the taste of tomatoes and most vegetable dishes.

Savory can be planted in open beds as soon as the weather permits. The

The Herb Garden

rows should be about 8″ to 10″ apart. If you want a later harvest, savory can be planted right up to the beginning of June. The gardener should cover the delicate seeds with a very thin layer of soil. As for the rest, this annual herb is hardy and undemanding.

Spice and Medicinal Properties: Savory has a strong, rather peppery fragrance and its leaves are rich in essential oil. This herb is soothing and makes heavy dishes more easily digestible.

Harvest and Use: The tender leaves can be picked all summer long. Shortly before and during its blooming season, however, savory reaches its highest concentration; this is when it can be cut and hung in bunches in a shady, well-ventilated place to dry. This herb has a fresh taste and goes well with soups, green beans, and potatoes.

Borage can be planted directly in open beds starting as early as April. These vigorous plants need a slightly moist soil rich in humus. The herb thrives in full sunlight as well as in partial shade; the plants are bushy and need a lot of room.

Spice and Medicinal Properties: The tender, soft leaves have a fresh but sour taste. The herb is rich in mucin, saponin, tannic and silicic acids. Borage is a cardiac stimulant and is said to have a positive effect on rheumatism.

Harvest and Use: Only the tender, young leaves should be picked and they should be used immediately. The blue flowers are also edible. Older plants turn coarse and firm, and the juicy leaves do not preserve well. Bor-

Borage is adorned with blue blossoms.

The seed pods of dill.

age makes a welcome addition to salads and cucumber dishes.

Dill is an indispensable herb. The seeds can be sown in the open in April and May. Dill loves a moist soil and thrives especially well in a cucumber bed where the long leaf tendrils protect the ground. Individual rows should be about 10″ to 12″ apart.

Spice and Medicinal Properties: Dill has its own unique, fresh fragrance. This herb is rich in essential oil and has a calming, soothing, and warming effect.

Harvest and Use: Dill leaves can be picked fresh as needed throughout the summer, and they can also be frozen. The blossoms and seeds are used to put up pickles. This spicy herb goes well with salads, cucumbers, and fish.

Chervil is an herb native to Europe and is not sensitive to cold. It can be planted in open beds as early as March. There should be about 4″ between the rows. Chervil grows rapidly and should be freshly reseeded rather frequently. The best location is partially shady and slightly moist.

Spice and Medicinal Properties: Chervil has a spicy-sweet taste somewhat reminiscent of anise. The leaves contain essential oil, glucosides, and bitter principles. It stimulates the metabolism.

Harvest and Use: Chervil leaves should be picked young and used fresh. This spicy herb adds to soups, omelets, and salads.

Cress is a rapidly growing, robust herb. The seeds can be planted in open beds as early as March, and the rows should be about 4″ apart. The seeds germinate within the first week; this herb is undemanding, and flourishes well even in partial shade.

Chervil should be picked when young and tender.

Spice and Medicinal Properties: Cress has a pungent and slightly sharp taste. It contains mustard oil, vitamin C, and bitter principles, and helps maintain digestive regularity.

Harvest and Use: Crest should always be cut and used fresh. During the winter months it can be cultivated on the windowsill in a small bowl filled with moist sand. Cress is used in salads, cottage cheese, with eggs and radishes.

Sweet Marjoram needs a great deal of warmth. The delicate seeds can be planted in May in the open garden and should be covered with only a thin layer of soil. Leave about 8″ to 10″ between the rows. This herb can also be cultivated in small pots. Marjoram prefers porous, sandy soil and a lot of sun.

Spice and Medicinal Properties: The little, round leaves give off an intense and spicy aroma. They contain a rich supply of essential oil as well as bitter

The Herb Garden

principles and tannin. Marjoram has a soothing yet stimulating effect on the stomach and is calming to the nerves.
Harvest and Use: Fresh leaves can be picked throughout the summer. This herb reaches its highest concentration shortly before the roundish blossoms open, and this is the best time to cut it for drying.

Biennial Herbs

Biennial herbs can be planted in spring and late summer. These herbs produce only leaves in their first year and blossoms and seeds in the following season.

Scurvy Grass is indigenous to the northern coast of Europe. It likes a somewhat moist soil, but is otherwise undemanding. The seedlings can be set as early as March, and the rows should be positioned about 8″ apart.
Spice and Medicinal Properties: Scurvy-grass leaves taste a bit like cress; they are slightly sharp and a little salty. The plants themselves are particularly rich in vitamin C and also contain mustard oil, tannin, and bitter principles.

This herb stimulates metabolism.
Harvest and Use: The spoon-shaped leaves can be harvested continuously. Since this is an evergreen herb, there is no need to preserve it. Scurvy grass is used in salads, with cottage cheese and egg dishes.
Parsley is the most familiar of all kitchen spices. It can be planted in open beds as early as March, and it prefers a rather moist soil rich in humus. The seeds germinate slowly, and the rows should be at least 4″ to 6″ apart. The smooth-leafed peasant

parsley is more fragrant and richer in vitamins than the popular curly-leafed varieties.
Spice and Medicinal Properties: Parsley has a strong, somewhat sharp and spicy taste. The leaves contain a good supply of essential oil and many vitamins. Parsley acts as a diuretic.
Harvest and Use: Parsley should always be picked fresh just prior to use. It is an evergreen herb and can thus be harvested continuously throughout the year. The leaves add flavor to potatoes, carrots, and other vegetables and are used in salads, sauces, and soups.

Perennial Herbs

Many spice plants belong to the family of perennial shrubs. They remain in place for years and reappear every spring. Perennial herbs can be purchased in gardening centers in the form of young plants, or they can be cultivated from seed, in which case

Parsley.

The Herb Garden

they should be transplanted to the open garden in spring or fall.

Tarragon needs a moist soil rich in humus. This herb thrives in direct sun as well as partial shade. The plants should be placed about 12″ to 15″ apart and they grow to a height of 2½′ to 5′. French tarragon is much more aromatic than Russian tarragon. These plants reproduce by means of root runners.

Spice and Medicinal Properties: Tarragon has a delicate fragrance with a touch of sweetness. The leaves contain essential oil, resin, tannin and bitter principles. This herb stimulates the appetite and acts as a diuretic.

Harvest and Use: Fresh young shoots can be harvested all summer long. Whole branches of tarragon can be dried just prior to the bloom. Since this herb is one of the epicurean spices, it is used in salads, sauces, herb butter, and fish dishes.

Lovage, with time, develops into a tall bush, sometimes 10′ in height. It needs a deep layer of humus and a lot of room. Lovage also thrives in partial shade.

Spice and Medicinal Properties: Lovage has a strong and pungent taste similar to that of soup spices. The leaves contain essential oil, resin, and bitter principles. They have a diuretic effect and relieve flatulence.

Harvest and Use: Tender, young leaves can be picked all summer long, but if you want to dry them, cut them just before the plants bloom. This strong-tasting herb makes its contribution to soups and sauces.

Mint loves sun and well-drained soil. The individual plants need about 12″ of space between them and can grow to a height of 19″ to 28″. Mint can be

Mint tastes like fresh lemons.

increased by dividing the plants.

Spice and Medicinal Properties: Mint leaves have a fresh and spicy taste similar to lemon. They contain essential oil, resin, tannin, and bitter principles. Mint calms the nerves and the heart.

Harvest and Use: Young leaves can be picked throughout the summer, and if this herb is to be dried for tea, it should be cut just prior to its bloom.

Fresh mint tastes very good in salads, sauces, cottage cheese, and tomato dishes.

Peppermint grows like a weed in moist, partially shady locations. It should therefore be planted only where it will not interfere with vegetables. There are many different varieties of mint, including pineapple, spearmint, and pennyroyal.

The Herb Garden

Spice and Medicinal Properties:
Everyone knows the taste of peppermint with its refreshing tinge of menthol. The leaves contain a rich supply of essential oil as well as tannin and bitter principles. Peppermint has a soothing and warming effect, and it helps relieve stomach discomfort and flatulence.

Harvest and Use: Fresh, young leaves can be picked all summer long. This herb should be cut and tied for drying shortly before the bloom. Dried peppermint leaves can be used as a tea. The fresh leaves go well with roast lamb, sauces, and summer drinks.

Sage likes a lot of sun and well-drained, somewhat limy soil. The plants need about 12″ to 15″ of space between them. They can be increased later by means of cuttings or shoots.

Spice and Medicinal Properties: The silver-gray leaves have a severe, camphorlike smell. They contain essential oil, resin, tannin, and bitter principles. Sage helps soothe sore throats, relieves bleeding of the gums and sweating during the night.

Sage is winter-hardy and has an attractive bloom.

Harvest and Use: Individual leaves can be picked at any time, but if you want to dry this herb, you should cut it shortly before the blue blossoms open. Sage is used with fish, ham, cheese, soups, and eels. The dried herb can also be used for a tea.

Thyme grows as a low ground cover. It needs a sunny location and sandy soil, and the individual plants should be placed 7″ to 8″ apart. In addition to the German and French varieties, there is also lemon thyme.

Spice and Medicinal Properties:
Thyme has a strong, spicy fragrance and is rich in essential oil. It also contains saponin, resin, tannin, and bitter principles.

This herb is antiseptic and relieves coughing and stomach cramps.

Harvest and Use: Thyme can be picked at any time of the year, but it should be cut just prior to the bloom if it is to be dried. It adds a distinctive flavor to fish, soups, sauces, and stews.

Hyssop loves the sun and a poor, somewhat limy soil. The plants should be 9″ to 12″ apart. They develop into bushes 15″ to 20″ tall and can be increased by planting individual cuttings.

Spice and Medicinal Properties: Hyssop has a pleasantly spicy, if somewhat bitter, taste. The leaves contain essential oil, resin, tannin, and bitter principles. It has a stimulating effect on the stomach and digestion process.

Harvest and Use: The tender leaves can be picked throughout the summer and whole branches can be dried shortly before the bloom. In small doses, hyssop has a special place in salads, sauces, ragouts, stews, and potato dishes.

The Strawberry Patch

Most gardens have no extra room for an honest-to-goodness fruit orchard. Sweet berries rich in vitamins, however, can be planted just about anywhere. They add to an organic garden with their nutritious fruits, which provide a healthy snack especially, but not exclusively, for children.

Organic gardeners will have no difficulties raising strawberries, raspberries, and currants. Once they become acquainted with the natural habitat of these plants, even beginning gardeners will soon become familiar with the necessary care.

The ancestors of our oversized strawberries are the small, aromatic wild strawberries found in forests and woods. Cross-cultivation has produced the meaty berries we know today. Despite all the changes they have undergone, these strawberry plants have not lost their preference for a slightly acidic soil rich in humus and a protected, sunny location. To predict what the plants in his or her garden will need, the organic gardener need only imagine for a moment the warm forest clearings where the strawberries grow.

A bed 4' wide had enough room for 2 rows of strawberry plants. The soil should be carefully prepared well in advance of planting. A generous amount of compost—preferably leaf compost—and an organic fertilizer should be mixed into the uppermost layer of the soil. Suitable for this pur-

A straw mulch proves its worth in the strawberry patch, for the fruit remains clean until picked.

The Strawberry Patch

pose are decayed dung and dried cow manure or horn-blood-and-bone meal. Even a stone meal that has no lime content can improve the soil in a strawberry patch. The final step again involves covering the whole bed with mulch.

The best time to plant is sometime in August or September. Strawberry plants should be placed in rows about 10″ to 12″ apart and the plant pit itself should be filled with an additional dose of ripe compost. Finally, the seedlings are best sprayed with a heavily diluted liquid stinging-nettle manure. A new mulch cover should be spread between the rows and should consist whenever possible of a slightly acidic material. Dead pine needles, mixed leaves, and bits of bark are especially recommended for this purpose. In this way organic gardeners re-create a bit of the old forest atmosphere for their own strawberry plants. These thrive especially well and grow vigorously under such natural conditions. The earth beneath the protective cover remains moist and loose. There is no need to rake; in fact, not raking allows the shallow strawberry roots to spread out undisturbed. If there is no leaf or peat mulch available, hay or cut grass can be used to cover the ground between the rows.

Organic gardeners can easily increase the number of strawberry plants if they learn to recognize the profusely productive mother plants in time. The runners of these plants should be removed during the sum-

Strawberry shoots form roots easily and can be planted directly into little pots in the bed. In this way the connection to the "mother" plant is not disturbed.

mer and planted on their own. A very practical way to do this is to bury small pots filled with a sandy humus mixture into the strawberry patch, and to press the runners, complete with their first roots, into these pots. The shoot can be held fast with a piece of bent wire, for the young plants should remain attached to their "mother" for a while at least. Strawberries rapidly form new roots, and the vigorous clumps in the pots make transplanting easier and facilitate growth in the eventual new beds.

After the harvest, adult strawberry plants should be given additional nutrients and compost because it is during the autumn weeks that the new shoots for next year's bloom are set. The roots, too, grow vigorously during this period. If the mulch cover has already begun to decay, it should be renewed before the onset of winter.

Under this sensible program of natural care, strawberry plants will flourish vigorously. The full fragrance of the berries will demonstrate to the organic gardener that he or she has tended the patch properly. Strawberries from an organic garden taste the way many people remember them from the happy days they spent in Grandmother's house.

The fragrance of the strawberry plant also plays a role in selecting the desired variety. Cultivars that produce large fruits trace the greatest part of their inheritance back to natives of Chile which have a lot of meat but little sweetness in their ancestry. This is one reason why the organic gardener should not immediately reach for the red miniberries. He or she should also pay particular attention to the aromatic cultivars.

A mulch of tansy leaves defends strawberries against slug attacks.

"Senga Sengana," for example, is a robust, worldwide aromatic variety which is known for producing fruit in rugged regions. Of the many other cultivars, the varieties "Macherauch's Marieva," "Regina," and the old favorite "Mieze Schindler" have a particularly pungent fragrance.

Those varieties of strawberries that bear fruit repeatedly throughout the summer and on into the fall are especially recommended for families with children. "Ostara" and "Imtraga" are very good examples and can be relied upon to produce the dainty, runnerless strawberries for weeks on end. In addition, they taste almost as sweet as wild strawberries.

In inclement weather, strawberry plants may be threatened by fungus diseases despite good care. Gray mold is particularly widespread. Organic gardeners can guard against damage from such diseases by strengthening their plants with a liquid stinging-nettle manure and by

Wild Berries in the Garden

spraying horsetail solution as a preventive measure. A mixed planting consisting of onions and garlic also tends to increase the strawberries' resistance to fungus diseases.

Raspberries and blackberries are among the sweet fruits of the forest that have gradually acclimated themselves to the home garden. They still grow wild in the form of underbrush in the light shade of protecting shrubs and trees. In the garden, as in their natural habitat, these berries like a light, acidic soil containing humus and a ground cover at their base.

A rich raspberry harvest.

Raspberries

The soil in raspberry beds should be well drained and as acidic as possible. Heavy soils have to be loosened with the help of compost and mulch. Sandy soils can be made more friable by adding stone meal and a generous amount of compost.

The best time to plant raspberries is in the fall or early spring. Place the young stalks against either a fence or a simple trellis. Posts at either end supporting 2 stretched wires will also suffice. There is no need to tie up the long shoots, for they can simply be wound about the wires.

If there are several rows of raspberries, a distance of at least 4' to 5' should be kept free between them. The individual plants should be placed about 15" to 24" apart because raspberries produce root runners in all directions. These new roots can be dug up and planted to produce additional individual specimens. The location should be prepared with compost, stone meal, and some organic fertilizer. Trim the roots a bit before planting, and plant the raspberries as low to the ground as possible. In the spring the shoots should be cut back to about 4 or 5 canes.

A mulch cover that must be continuously renewed throughout the whole year is very important for the healthy growth of raspberries. Especially well suited for this purpose are slightly acidic substances such as leaves, dead pine needles, bits of bark, wood shavings, and pulverized sticks and branches. Nevertheless, a green manure beneath the raspberries has an excellent effect as a living ground cover. Use predominantly papiliona-

Wild Berries in the Garden

ceous plants for this purpose. Frozen leaves should remain on the ground throughout the winter. Anthracnose, one of the most virulent fungus infections, can usually be warded off successfully by a natural ground cover. Nevertheless, at the first sign of this disease the affected branches should be removed and burned to prevent the disease from spreading.

Raspberries bear their fruit on the twigs that were set during the previous summer and survived the winter. As soon as the harvest is over, the spent branches should be cut back to the ground. Each plant should retain between 5 and 7 of the most vigorous new shoots, and all the remaining weaker ones should be removed. In the case of those varieties that bear more than one crop of fruit, the gardener must naturally wait until the second harvest is over in the fall. Raspberry plants that are carefully trimmed and given this sort of natural care remain healthy and produce sweet, fragrant fruit.

Blackberries

Blackberries, which ripen on vigorous and thorny twigs, are particularly nutritious and rich in vitamins. They grow like raspberries under similar conditions, but are more vigorous and more robust. The soil preparations are the same. Blackberries, too, need a constant mulch cover.

Organic gardeners should set blackberry bushes a little bit deeper in the ground than raspberries. The best time to plant is between March and April. These vigorously growing bushes should be placed far apart:

those that grow upright need about 3' to 5' between them, while the creeping varieties need between 10' and 14' free space. The young blackberry shoots can be cut back after planting to about 8" or 12".

An important element for a manageable blackberry patch is a stable trellis accessible from both sides. It can be easily constructed out of 2 strong posts serving as supports for several connecting wires. The long, thorny branches should be guided by and tied to these wires. Only a regular pruning, however, will prevent this blackberry trellis from turning into an impenetrable thicket. This is why organic gardeners usually permit only 6 young shoots to grow from each rootstock in any one year, and these shoots have to be immediately and carefully tied to the support structure. Every weak branch should be removed. The lateral branches that grow from the axils of the main stems have to be cut back in the summertime to 1 or 2 buds. In late summer, after the harvest, all spent branches should be severed from the main trunk very close to the ground. You can get a very good overview of the fruit-bearing branches as well as of the young new shoots if the blackberries are firmly fastened to a double espalier—the old branches attached to one side, and the young new shoots attached to the other.

By taking and setting new shoots, an organic gardener can easily increase the number of blackberry bushes in his or her garden. Simply bend a branch toward the ground and press it into the soil. New roots will develop at this point, and the new plant can then be separated from the

Berry Bushes

parent, dug out, and transplanted in another location.

There are also thornless varieties available among the many new blackberry cultivars, one of which is called "Thornless Evergreen." The vigorously growing blackberries are generally less susceptible to disease than are raspberries. A dose of liquid stinging-nettle manure does them a lot of good. As for the rest, they tend to grow well and produce profusely for years if given the natural care they need.

Gooseberries and currants are indigenous to northern and central Europe. They used to grow wild in open meadows and along the edges of forests with a thick and colorful carpet of herbs and grasses covering the soil above their roots. If organic gardeners keep this picture in mind, they will have no trouble in finding the proper place in the garden for berry bushes: sunny to partially shady, and protected from harsh winds.

Red and White Currants

Currants can grow in the light shade of fruit trees or ornamental shrubs. Nevertheless, a sufficient amount of direct sunshine must be able to filter through so that the berries can ripen and become sweet.

The organic gardener should carefully prepare the location of the bushes in good time prior to planting. The soil must be deep and loose, for these bushes remain in the same place for many years and produce abundant yields of berries. One worthwhile approach is to plant the area with a deep-rooting green manure a good deal in advance of the arrival of the berry bushes. Working the soil after the bushes are in place is no longer possible, because the shallow and expansive roots of the bushes should not be disturbed.

Dig a hole large enough to accommodate the entire root system comfortably. Compost and stone meal can then be mixed into this hole. Currants should be planted a bit deeper than they originally were in the nursery, because this tends to encourage the growth of many new shoots in the soil. The branches above ground can be cut back ⅔ their length after the bush is accustomed to its new home. The best time to arrange a new berry patch is in late fall or early spring. The distance between individual currant bushes should range between 4½' and 6'.

Mature bushes can be tended in the fall or early spring with compost and an organic fertilizer such as horn-blood-and-bone meal or ground limestone. They will also welcome a spraying of liquid stinging-nettle manure. The most important thing for healthy growth, however, is a layer of mulch that should cover the ground beneath the bushes throughout the year. The organic gardener can use woody debris, leaves, hay, nettle cuttings, comfrey leaves, or a green manure for this purpose.

Both red and white currants bear their fruit on 2-to-3-year-old wood. For one bush, 8–12 strong shoots will suffice. Every year after the harvest or in the fall the gardener should remove those branches that are more than 4 years old by cutting them back very

Berry Bushes

close to the ground. They can be recognized by their dark color. 2 or 3 strong new shoots should be allowed to develop in their stead. The weak and young branches that bear too profusely can be removed, as well as those that cross one another or grow inward toward the main trunks. In this way the currant bush always keeps its shape; it will have a loose and airy appearance, and the rays of sun can penetrate completely, which is an important prerequisite for healthy and vigorous growth. If the atmosphere is suffocatingly humid, on the other hand, diseases and insect pests can easily attack.

In addition to the berry bushes, there are currant trees and the somewhat shorter shrubs. The attractive little trees with branched trunks are especially appropriate for small gardens. They can be planted along a path, for example, without being overshadowed by neighboring plants. The tops of these trees should be trimmed in keeping with the growth patterns of the bushes. The only additional care the organic gardener has here is to shape the crown attractively.

Wormwood planted between currant bushes will protect them against rust. Organic gardeners can also spray them with a wormwood solution. Preventive treatment with horsetail solutions protects against fungus diseases.

Black Currants

These bushes can be recognized by their smell. If you rub the wood between your fingers, you will smell the unmistakable aroma of black currants. The bushes are to be planted in keeping with the same guidelines described for red currants. However, these plants need 6'–8' of open space between them, for they tend to grow vigorously. Black currants prefer a moist soil and they can tolerate some shade.

The most important difference has

Pruning the canes of a berry bush.

Cutting back the roots before planting.

to do with trimming these plants:
Black currants bear their fruit on 1-year-old wood. Organic gardeners should thus prune these bushes regularly. Every year after the harvest the spent branches should be cut back to the ground, and 2 or 3 new shoots may be allowed to grow in their stead. As a rule, this bush should consist of no more than 8 main branches, so that air and sunlight can reach all parts of the bush at all times. Like their red and white relatives, black currants, too, come in the form of ornamental trees with branched trunks.

If the currants should become infested with gall mites, organic gardeners can fight back by spraying with tansy tea (see recipe, p. 61). In extreme cases they can also resort to pyrethrum preparations.

Gooseberries

These thorny bushes with the sweet-and-sour fruit thrive under conditions similar to those preferred by currant plants. They are fairly undemanding, can tolerate some shade, but are particularly fond of soils that contain both lime and loam. A distance of about 4½' should be kept free between the individual gooseberry bushes. 3½' to 4' will suffice between the small, ornamental varieties with branched trunks. These trees need a support pole and a trellis to protect branches heavily laden with fruit from breaking off.

Planting a currant tree: a large pit, a support pole, and a woody mulch cover.

Flowers from Seed

Many gardeners who have changed over to natural methods still believe that organic gardens should feature only food plants. This is an illogical assumption, for in nature itself trees, berry bushes, wild vegetables, herbs, and flowers all thrive together in keeping with the same fundamental principles. The same holds true for the organic garden. Compost, organic fertilizers, and liquid stinging-nettle manure also ensure the healthy growth of roses, ornamental bushes and shrubs, and summer flowers. Even the principle of ground covers can be applied in the flower garden to a certain extent.

The neat division between a vegetable and an ornamental garden is an invention of the bourgeois mentality. Once in a while organic gardeners should use the old-fashioned farmer's garden as a model, for here flowers and vegetables grow happily and healthily in motley confusion. They share the same friable soil, and their combination is of advantage to both the useful and the ornamental. The greatest economy as well as the greatest joys of a summer garden spring almost exclusively out of small seed packages. With home-grown flowers such as these, our organic gardener can turn his or her prosaic plot into a

In just a few weeks annual summer flowers explode into color.

Flowers from Seed

magical wonderland. This beauty, however, is ephemeral. The short-lived children of Flora unfold and evolve within the course of a few brief weeks in the summer, only to perish with the onset of the first frost.

Annual Summer Flowers

April or May is the time for organic gardeners to plant annual summer flowers in open beds. Sensitive species, however, are better cultivated on a warm windowsill, in a hotbed, or in a small greenhouse. The outdoor seedbed ought to be well prepared, loose, and friable. Ideally, it should be tended in the previous fall by adding compost, stone meal, and a time-released or slowly acting organic fertilizer composed of horn-blood-

Sunflowers are very picturesque.

and-bone meal. Once spring has come, the organic gardener can divide the bed into rows and label with seed packages the names of the flowers that will soon grace each row.

The varying summer-flower seeds should be distributed and lightly covered with a thin layer of soil or ripe compost. Try not to plant them too close together, for the growing plants will need room to spread out. It is essential to water the seedbed regularly. During very warm, dry weeks in spring an old, wet jute sack can be placed over the bed to help keep it moist. It should be removed as soon as the first germinal leaves poke through the soil.

Several robust varieties of summer flowers can be sown broadcast directly into the garden bed, but it is always best to follow the directions on the back of the individual seed packages.

Toward the end of May, when the individual plants have had a chance to develop somewhat, you can transplant them to their final location in the garden. Remember to keep enough open space between them so that they can branch out at will.

These annual flowers can be used to fill in holes in an herb garden or they can be used to form entire beds or borders. They thrive in front of ornamental bushes and on the edges of vegetable gardens. Wherever they are, they always need a great deal of direct sunlight. In shady locations or under otherwise restricted conditions, these annual beauties never realize their full potential.

Organic gardeners should pay some attention to the ultimate height of the various plants and make sure the

Flowers from Seed

combinations he or she has chosen will blend together to make a harmonious whole. A skilled gardener can work like an artist with the translucent colors of summer flowers. The right color combinations can produce graceful and charming garden scenes.

Once the soil has been well prepared with compost and an autumnal green manure, all that is needed is one or two additional and substantial sprayings of liquid stinging-nettle manure during the main growing season. This should be done, however, only after the plants have taken a good hold in their new location. Summer flowers should produce as many blossoms as possible; if the gardener gives them too much nourishment, they tend to develop too many "fat leaves" and lose their ability to bloom. If, on the other hand, the organic gardener regularly removes all wilted blossoms, he or she will already have done the most important thing to encourage weeks of profuse blooming.

A small selection of the many flowers available in seed packages may make the gardener's choice a bit easier.

Asters rank among the most popular of all summer flowers. They can be planted in open beds as early as April. On the other hand, if they are left to germinate in a hotbed, they tend to bloom a bit earlier than otherwise. When making your choice among the many available varieties, be sure to consider the wilt-resistant cultivars. Asters bloom in many colors and come in dwarf form as well as medium-sized and tall varieties.

Annual summer flowers: violet old-fashioned funnel mallow (above), gaillardia (middle), and an iridescent zinnia (below).

Garden Cornflowers are undemanding and bloom profusely in blue, violet, and pink. Depending upon the variety, they can attain a height of 15" to 39".

Summer Fuchsias introduce romanticism into your summer garden. They bloom in shades of pale pink, white, and red and make very pretty bouquets. With their 15" to 20", they rank among the middle class as far as height is concerned. There are many varieties, with wide variations in color.

Snapdragons belong in a farmer's garden! It pays to cultivate these flowers in the warmth, for then the velvety blossoms will brighten the whole summer with warm shades of red, pink, orange, yellow, and white. Snapdragons can grow to a height of 3'.

Marigolds, too, belong in every organic garden, and they are as pretty as they are practical. The large seed pods germinate easily, and once they have made themselves at home, they tend to reseed themselves from year to year. Marigolds are usually 12" to 19" tall.

Cosmos form bushes 3' to 5' in height with delicately pinnate foliage. The simple, cup-shaped flowers glow pink, red, or white.

Sunflowers are to a summer garden what stars are to a summer sky. They can be sown directly into open beds, but the mighty flowers should ideally be given something to lean against, such as a fence or a wall. They also need more nourishment than other summer flowers.

Black-eyed Susans introduce a certain mood into the garden. The iridescent yellow or rust-brown flowers with

You can plant wild cornflowers (above) right from the seed packet as well as strawflowers (middle) and cosmos (below).

104

Flowers from Seed

the black "hat" in the center are very durable and can attain a height of 2' to 3'. **Strawflowers** prolong the summer right into winter. These long-lasting blossoms can be bunched together and hung up to dry. There are medium-sized and tall varieties, which can reach a height of 30".

Like the marigolds, the related variety known as **French Marigolds** are one of the "weapons" in an organic garden. They can be cultivated easily, either in hotbeds or in open gardens. Unfortunately, slugs consider these flowers their favorite dish. The young plants must therefore be especially well protected. These flowers bloom incessantly until the first frost in luminous shades of gold, brown, and rust.

Old-fashioned **Funnel Mallows** are charming, rustic flowers. They can be sown directly into the garden bed and bloom for weeks on end. The open blossoms have the appearance of pink or white silk.

Zinnias are best cultivated in a hotbed, and the large blossoms with their stiff stems are always grateful for a shower of liquid stinging-nettle manure. The zinnia blossoms are particularly long-lasting. There are small-blossomed varieties as well as magnificent cultivars that playfully attain a height of 3'.

Hollyhocks lend old-fashioned charm.

Mulleins have a majestic appearance.

Biennial Summer Flowers

Somewhat longer-lived than the annual beauties are the biennial flowers. They should be sown in the summer, June or July, and then transplanted in the fall; they will begin to bloom, though, only in the following year. The same rules that govern

Flowers from Seed

Foxglove fits in well in natural gardens.

the annuals apply for the seeding, soil preparation, and transplanting of these summer flowers. The biennials, however, should not be fertilized until the following spring.

Among these plants with a life rhythm of 2 and sometimes even more years can be found many of the old, rustic garden flowers that blend in very well in any organic garden. If you are patient and observant, you will be able to stimulate these plants to a longer life span. They will then reward you with a third year of blossoms.

Sweet Williams are also known as Carthusian pinks. The flat blossoms with their spicy fragrance are arranged in thick, rustic corymbs. These old-fashioned carnations bloom white, pink, or red. There are dwarf varieties for borders and tall cultivars that can reach a height of about 20".

Foxglove or **Digitalis** introduces a touch of the forest into the garden. Besides the purplish-pink natural form there are beautiful cultivars in various colors. Foxglove blends in well with wild-flower arrangements in organic gardens.

Wallflowers smell like no other flower. The velvety blossoms in gold and warm reddish-brown tones were already at home in cloister and peasant gardens centuries ago. There are double as well as single-blossom varieties.

Common Mulleins are truly majestic flowers that grow between 4½' and 6' tall. The original forms can also be integrated into herb gardens, since they rank among the ancient medicinal plants. Moreover, there are beautiful new cultivars that add luster and brilliance to bushes and shrubs.

Pansies are not difficult to grow from seed. They are a beautiful, living ground cover. They frequently begin to bloom in the fall, and are not damaged by cold.

Hollyhocks are frequently 6' to 10'. They flourish when leaning against a fence or wall and need a lot of room, sun, and nutrients. Favorable location and sufficient moisture protect them against rust, as do sprayings with horsetail solutions.

Advantages of Bushes and Shrubs

Garden Bushes Are Members of the Old Guard

The organic gardener is well advised to prepare the soil in his or her shrub garden very thoroughly before planting. It pays to dig up every weed by the roots, because it can become a source of irritation later on if bushes and weeds grow hopelessly entangled in one another.

The soil can be improved prior to planting by adding a generous amount of compost and a slow-working organic fertilizer. Although these plants do need nourishment, they should never be overfed, for this leads to more foliage than flowers. The best time to plant the perennial varieties is in the cool months of September and October and in the early spring—March or April. In deciding where to

The art of a shrub garden rests in the harmonious combination of plants.

Delphiniums bloom in early summer.

The sweet fragrance of phlox heralds the height of summer.

place the young plants, organic gardeners should always consider the ultimate dimensions of the mature plant, for this will determine the distance between the individual bushes and shrubs. The eventual height of the flowering plants must also be kept in mind. "Giants" like delphiniums should be planted toward the back, whereas the broad middle expanse can accommodate the medium-sized specimens like daisies and phlox. The lower varieties can then take their place in the foreground.

The varying blooming seasons as well as the different colors also call for skillful combination. Borders or beds have a particularly pleasing effect if several representatives of a single species are planted together. In this way you establish peaceful islands within a turbulent sea of blossoms.

In caring for a bed of this description, it is important that the soil be open and friable. It ought to be loosened and fertilized in the fall. And don't forget that you will need room to trim the bushes and water the plants. In order to prevent a newly arranged bush-and-shrub bed from drying out, organic gardeners may plant summer flowers wherever there is an empty spot. This has the additional advantage of rapidly consolidating the ground cover. These annual ground plants should be removed in the fall, and the bed is now ready for a repetition of the above-described preparation process.

Asters grow in the form of tall (about 4½') or short (8" to 16") bushes that are smothered with profuse, starlike blossoms. These plants need a soil rich in humus and a great deal of

Advantages of Bushes and Shrubs

sunlight. There are very robust, coarse-leafed varieties as well as smooth-leafed ones that frequently suffer from mildew. The blooming season lasts from September to October.

Chrysanthemums are indigenous to Asia and rank among the oldest of garden flowers. These sober-smelling plants produce the last blossoms of the fall. Even in frost they glow with white, pink, red, yellow, and brown colors. Chrysanthemums need a good soil, abundant nutrients, and sun. They can grow to a height of 16" to 40". The best time to plant is spring, and their blooming season lasts from August to November.

Goldenrod comes in loose bushes with bright yellow panicles. It's undemanding, can tolerate partial shade, and grows between 16" and 40" tall. Blooming period: July to October.

Iris or **Fleur-de-lis** blooms in all colors of the rainbow. It needs a well-drained soil and full sunlight. There are enchanting new cultivars of these ancient plants: dwarf irises are only 8" high; taller varieties can easily attain a height of 3'. Organic gardeners can collect the seeds of the fleur-de-lis themselves and thus be assured of an ample supply. The best time to plant is June to September, and the blooming season lasts from May to June.

Japanese Anemones thrive in light shade. They need a porous but moist soil. The delicate, porcelainlike blossoms in white or pink transform the garden in late summer. These graceful shrubs can grow 13" to 39" tall. Blooming season is August to October.

Lupines with their tall, candle-shaped blossoms brighten up the whole gar-

A trampoline for bees: asters.

den. They need a soil rich in humus and thrive as well in direct sun as in partial shade. These plants grow to a height of 30" to 45", and their blooming season extends from May to July.

Daisies with their white blossoms are a must in every garden. They prefer a humus soil, but are otherwise undemanding. These plants usually grow 20" to 40" tall. Their blooming season ranges from July to August.

Poppies are an Oriental splendor. The large, silky blossoms come in shades of iridescent red, pink, or white. These plants can grow to a height of 20" to 40" and need a soil rich in humus and lime as well as direct sun. Blooming season is from May to June.

Peonies have been cultivated for thousands of years. There are cultivars with Chinese ancestors as well as the old European peasant peony. These bushes should not be planted too deep in the ground, and they do not take kindly to transplanting. Peonies prefer a somewhat limy humus soil and a lot of sun. The red, pink, or

Advantages of Bushes and Shrubs

Peonies are old and elegant garden flowers.

white varieties can grow as tall as 20″ to 40″. Their blooming period lasts from May to June.

Phlox is one of the most beautifully fragrant of all summer shrubs. It needs a good, nutrient-containing garden soil and a lot of direct sun. The profuse blossoms come in shades of white, pink, red, and lilac. These

A glorious cactus dahlia.

plants usually range between 28″ and 60″ tall, and their blooming season extends from June to September.

Delphiniums are always the center of attraction in any bush-and-shrub garden. The brilliant blue as well as white flower "towers" can range between 30″ and 70″ tall and need a soil rich in humus, ample nutrients, a lot of water, and direct, full sunlight. Their main blooming season is June to July and they also bloom again from September to October.

Bleeding Hearts are enchanting, old-fashioned plants that like some shade and moist soil. They can grow about 30″ tall and bloom from May to June.

Dahlias grow from fleshy tubers that are not winter-hardy. They must be dug up and stored in the cellar in moist peat before being replanted in open beds the following May. They need a nutrient-containing humus soil and sun. There are many varieties and species ranging from the dainty Mignon dahlia to the large-blossomed cactus and ornamental dahlias. Blooming season: July to October.

Gladioli enrich the garden bed and produce durable cut flowers. These fall plants (24″ to 48″ tall) develop from bulbs that should be planted in the spring about 4″ deep. They prefer a light soil and much sunlight, and the bulbs have to be taken in for the winter months. Blooming season: July to September.

Madonna Lilies are noble old garden flowers that give off a sweet fragrance. The bulbs should be planted in August in such a way that they lie only about 1″ below the surface of the ground. If these lilies have a well-drained soil and direct sun, they can grow to a height of 6′.

Advantages of Bushes and Shrubs

Wild Shrubs for Natural Gardens

The group of plants commonly called wild shrubs do not by any means originate in the wilderness. They are as commercially available as any other type of plant. The only difference, however, is that, although they have been cultivated, their basic characteristics have not been altered in any way. They still possess much of the natural charm of their forefathers.

Unlike the bed bushes, wild bushes and shrubs thrive well in community plantings that tend to grow densely together with time and thus form ground covers. Once this happens, they need very little additional attention. This type of natural "community" blends especially well into an organic garden. The gardener should become better acquainted with these plants and their companions in order to combine them for pleasing and lasting arrangements. The following pages will offer suggestions that can easily be put into practice.

The first step is to thoroughly prepare the place that is intended to become the home for these plants for years to come. The soil should be deeply loosened and free of weeds. A generous amount of compost and a slow-working organic fertilizer can then be added. One suggestion would be a horn-blood-and-bone-meal mixture.

The best time to set up a wild bush-and-shrub garden is in the fall because this is also the time to plant the bulbs for summer flowers. The organic gardener should adhere to the following procedure:

First, distribute loosely or in small

Bulb flowers and wild shrubs get along well together.

Advantages of Bushes and Shrubs

groups the bulbs of the spring bloomers that are meant to blend with wilder specimens. These include, among others, narcissus, snowdrops, bluebells, wild crocuses, and anemones. A few of the lower-growing varieties of cultivated tulips also work well here.

The perennial wild shrubs should be positioned between these plants, arranged in keeping with their height and color. Since all the plants are still lying loose on the ground, the gardener can easily shift them around to make sure they will not be in each other's way.

Once a compatible and pleasing community has been arranged, the actual planting can begin. Start with

the wild shrubs, followed by the flower bulbs in the intervening spaces.

As a last step, organic gardeners usually scatter some ground covers over the free surfaces beneath which he or she has just planted the small bulbs. With time, these low-growing plants will cover the whole area with a living carpet. The bulb plants have no trouble in penetrating this cover; rather, it gives them a sense of security and protection. And no garden rake will ever inadvertently chop them to bits.

During the first two years, organic gardeners should tend this new bed carefully so that no unwelcome weeds join forces with the shrubs to form an

Wild shrubs grow in dense clumps and need little care.

Advantages of Bushes and Shrubs

mpenetrable thicket. Once the plant cover is in place, the gardener has very little to do. As in their native habitat, the wild shrubs of this community will take care of themselves.

One important element in this vigorous and durable garden bed, however, is the proper choice of plants for the proper location. In other words, it behooves our organic gardener to learn to distinguish between shrubs that prefer direct sunlight and those that thrive in partial shade. The following selection is meant to be of assistance in finding the most compatible neighbors.

Wild Shrubs for Dry, Sunny Locations

Tall thistles, globe thistles, Siberian irises, yarrow, day lilies, and speedwell make up the taller members of this group. Common mullein can also be included. Grayish-blue brush grasses supplement this dry society: blue wild rye, blue fescue, and other ornamental grasses also gravitate toward sunny locations.

Good ground covers include heather, thyme, catnip, helianthemum.

Wild Shrubs for Moist, Partially Shady Spots

Columbine, astilbe, pink cloveroot, primroses, storksbill, and meadowsweet as well as foxglove (digitalis)

Hedge nettles and bluebells.

are all at home in this company. In addition, you can include ferns and forest grasses such as sedge grass and wood rush.

The following plants can be used as a ground cover: wood anemones, liverwort, lungwort, comfrey, violets, lilies of the valley, and woodruff.

Roses

Roses have been the gardener's favorite flower since time immemorial. Chinese emperors and Oriental potentates have let themselves be enchanted by these noble and fragrant blossoms as much as any courtly lady in any medieval cloister garden. Nor can modern organic gardeners resist the charm of these flowers. They should be tended, however, slightly differently than is the case in many home gardens.

Roses are by nature medium-sized, woody bushes. In open landscapes, dog roses are surrounded by a graceful combination of grasses and blooming wild flowers. A beginning organic gardener should keep this in mind if he or she intends to plant roses and wants to arrange them agreeably in a natural garden.

A monoculture that features as many flowering "prima donnas" as possible all crowded together in a single restricted bed does not correspond in any way to the conceptions of an organic garden. Even the widespread custom of cutting roses way back every year and trimming them to a uniform height goes against the grain of natural growing conditions.

Organic gardeners should therefore endeavor to let their roses grow in small bushes as nature intended. Moreover, they can spare this queen of the flower kingdom boring monotony and instead provide her with diverting company by planting their roses in a cheerful community that also includes shrubs and grasses.

Particularly appropriate for gardens with a "natural" emphasis are those species or varieties of roses that still display a little of their original character. Their sweet fragrance, for example, is inseparable from the image of noble, blooming rosebushes. Many modern cultivars, however, can offer only a pretty form; the fragrance has been lost somewhere along the path of horticultural crossbreeding. And with it the flowers have lost a portion of their incomparable magic.

One of the great advantages of modern rose cultivation is the fact that the newer cultivars bloom more profusely and more frequently than ever before. The horticulturist of our century has succeeded in prolonging the blooming season well into the fall, and this has increased the enjoyment these beautiful, durable, and varied flowers can provide.

In choosing specific roses, organic gardeners should consider both sides of the coin: the fragrance and many an alluring and nostalgic blossom from the good old days versus the profusion of bloom and resistance to disease of modern cultivars. Good, well-stocked nurseries offer a selection of old, historic roses as well as the new cultivars and wild varieties. The selection is so extensive that even an organic gardener can find the proper plants for his or her natural garden. The following brief descriptions are only meant to scratch the surface. In the course of time, organic gardeners will be able to call upon their own experiences and use them to decide upon the varieties and species that most appeal to their personal taste.

Tea Roses produce large, magnificently formed individual blossoms, and they make very good cut roses. The following varieties are distinguished by their combination of beauty and fragrance: "Erotica" (vel-

Snow White'' and ''Paderborn'' roses need room to spread out.

vety deep red); "First Lady" (pale pink); "Duftwolke" (reddish-orange); "Papa Meilland" (dark red); "Prima Ballerina" (cherry red); "Whiskey" (yellowish-bronze).

Grandiflora, Polyantha, and **Floribunda Roses** bloom in luxuriant bunches. They are also known as bed roses because they can be combined and planted in groups. The color effect in the garden is more brilliant and more varied here than is the case with tea roses, and this is due to the profusion of their bloom. There are innumerable cultivars, of which only a few can be mentioned here: "Lilli Marlene" (fiery red); "Irish Beauty" (salmon red, fragrant); "Orange Sen-

Roses

sation'' (bright reddish-orange, fragrant); ''Prominent'' (orange, fragrant); ''Queen Elizabeth'' (silvery pink); ''Frisia'' (golden yellow, fragrant)

Old Historical Roses enchant the onlooker with their thick, round double blossoms and their unforgettable, intense fragrance. The few examples that follow are intended to lead to individual experiments: ''Mrs. John Laing'' (pale pink); ''Souvenir De La Malmaison'' (creamy white with a tinge of pink); ''Queen of Denmark'' (silvery pink with a dark center); ''Panachée Double'' (pink and white stripes); ''Reines des Violettes'' (violet)

Climbing and **Rambler Roses** have to be securely attached to espaliers or wire support structures. They climb along house walls or over rose trellises and come in many different varieties, including ''New Dawn'' (porcelain pink, fragrant); ''Sympathie'' (dark red, fragrant); ''Leverkusen'' (bright yellow, fragrant).

Shrub and **Wild Roses** are particularly appropriate for natural gardens. The organic gardener can choose from a large selection of species and varieties that have preserved their wildflower characteristics. These roses grow tall and need a lot of room for their overhanging branches. A brief peek into the rich world of these domesticated flowers: *Rosa centifolia* ''Muscosa'' (spicy, fragrant, pink moss rose); *Rosa hugonis* (golden yellow, single-blossomed China rose); *Rosa lutea* ''Bicolor Altropurpurea'' (scentless reddish-yellow rose); ''C. F.

Old-fashioned roses like the Bourbon rose (above) fit in well in natural gardens. ''Queen Elizabeth'' (below) produces noble blossoms.

Meyer'' (a pink-colored, fragrant rose).
Rose Ground Covers and **Trailing
Roses** are a result of horticultural
crossbreeding. They grow flat and
cover the ground with blooming tendrils. These roses are well suited for
plantings in natural gardens. Recom-
mendations: "Fleurette" (carmine
red); "Heidenröslein-Nozomi"(mother-
of-pearl pink); "Max Graf" (pink).

Planting

The first step in the planting process
involves selecting a good location for
your roses. Small as well as large
bushes need a lot of sunshine, and a
loamy, humous soil is just about ideal
for their root systems. Light, sandy
soils ought to be improved with generous doses of compost and stone
meal. All heavy, nonporous clay soils
become looser when sand is mixed
into them. Of course, compost, too,
has to be added. Contrary to a widely
held belief, peat contributes nothing
to a rose bed. If it is regularly applied,
the soil turns sour and thus nonbene-
ficial for this Queen of Flora.

Good, decayed cow manure is the
best fertilizer for roses. But since it is
seldom available, the organic gardener should use dried cow manure
or a horn-blood-and-bone-meal combination fertilizer. The bed in which
the roses are to be planted should be
thoroughly loosened a few weeks in
advance, weeded, mixed with compost and dung, and then covered with
a layer of mulch. The best time to

How to plant roses: Water them thoroughly
(above); cut back the roots (middle); and
bury the bud union below the surface of the
ground (below).

Roses

Ready for winter: protection of dirt and leaves.

plant is during the autumn months of October and November and again in the spring, March and April.

The plant pits should be large and deep enough for the roots to spread out comfortably. It is always best to soak the roots in a pail of water prior to planting. After they have been left to soak for a few hours, the roots should be cut back by ⅓ with a pair of garden clippers. The branches, however, should be trimmed only during the spring.

The soil that was removed to dig the holes should be thoroughly mixed with compost and stone meal and then used to cover the roots and hold them in place. It ought to be stamped down rather firmly, so that all the roots come into contact with it. As a final step, organic gardeners always generously water their newly planted roses. If everything is done properly, the grafting spot, which looks like a knot on the root system, should be 2″ below ground. The individual plants should be far enough apart that their branches will be able to develop without interference from a neighboring bush. If roses are planted too close to one another, the plants can easily fall victim to disease.

Trimming

All roses should be trimmed in the spring, but in a natural garden bed roses should not be cut back too severely. Our organic gardener first removes all frozen twigs and all branches that are growing inward. He or she should then cut the main shoots back, but by ⅓ at the most. The objective is to give the rosebushes a loose and airy appearance. Always cut on an angle and right above a cane that is directed outward.

Only newly planted roses need be vigorously trimmed back to ⅓ of their original height in the first spring. Shrub and bush roses usually come under the category of ornamental shrubs. These should never be cut back, but rather allowed to develop freely and naturally. Only the frozen wood and aged branches need be cut back to the ground. Branches and twigs that are growing toward the center or that are keeping air and light from the rest of the bush should also be removed. Tall-climbing varieties of rambler roses should be tended in the same way, but the organic gardener's only task here is to make sure that these roses do not proliferate wildly but are still able to put out new shoots continuously.

Care

Roses need a generous dose of nutrients twice a year—early in the

Roses with mildew.

Rust on rose leaves.

spring and again after their first main blooming in early summer. In addition to cow manure and horn-blood-and-bone meal, the organic gardener can also use wood ashes, guano, organic fertilizers, and a liquid stinging-nettle manure. From August on, all fertilizing should stop because the wood has to have a chance to mature. When these deeply rooted plants need watering during dry summer weeks, organic gardeners let the water flow directly and generously over the root area. They know that sprinkling systems damage roses because the dripping water injures the blossoms and makes the wet leaves susceptible to fungus infections in warm weather. It is a good idea to remove all withered blossoms regularly. Such "cleaned up" roses do not waste their strength producing seeds; rather, they use it to set profuse new buds promptly.

Roses can be protected against winter frost by piling compost or earth around their trunks. In areas known for very rugged weather conditions, the bushes can be loosely covered with spruce or pine branches.

Organic Plant Protection

The best prevention program consists of the natural care of the soil. Prophylactic sprayings with horsetail solutions and some commercially available preparations help ward off fungus diseases such as rust or mildew. Garlic between the bushes and a mulch cover made from tea leaves tend to strengthen roses against these infections.

Organic gardeners can keep lice and aphids under reasonable control if they spray with a caustic liquid stinging-nettle manure or dust the leaves with algal limestone. Lavender, when planted next to roses, also had a defensive effect against lice. Only in

(Not Merely Ornamental) Shrubs

extreme situations should organic gardeners resort to pyrethrum preparations or soft-soap solutions.

Mixed Plantings

Organic gardeners usually combine roses with blue delphiniums, pink gysophila, white Madonna lilies, and white daisies. Ornamental sage, lavender, and veronica also blend well with a motley-colored rose garden.

Woody plants provide the fixed and lasting framework for any garden. Their luxuriant blossoms or attractive leaves contribute greatly to the beauty of their surroundings. They are also indispensable, however, because of their practical qualities. Shrub hedges not only shield the garden from the glance of curious onlookers; they also screen noise and dust. And in a natural garden they have an additional function to fulfill: Their dense branches serve as home base for many different kinds of birds. Their berries provide natural nourishment for man and beast alike, and in the leaves and branches below the shrubs small creatures find a protected environment in which to live and work.

Wherever possible, then, gardens with a natural emphasis should feature these useful and protective hedges. Suitable for this purpose is a whole series of ornamental shrubs that make an undeniably attractive addition when they burst into bloom in the springtime and bedeck themselves with bright fruit in the fall.

Hedges such as these consist of loosely spaced individual shrubs. They should be planted at least 4½′ inside the property line so that their overhanging branches do not encroach upon the neighbor's garden.

For the preparation of the soil, organic gardeners can follow the same guidelines that apply for berry bushes. The best time to plant the deciduous varieties is in late autumn. (October to November). If the shrub is purchased with a root ball, the cloth that binds the roots should be cut and removed. The "naked" roots are then trimmed somewhat with a sharp knife. The branches of these woody plants should also be cut back slightly.

The shrubs themselves should be planted at least as deeply as they were in the nursery or garden center, but not so deeply that the soil is piled up around their trunks. The plant pit can be refilled with the soil that was dug out to make the hole, and it should be carefully and firmly stamped down over the roots. The final step is to water generously and cover the ground surrounding the shrubs with a layer of mulch.

The shrubs described and recommended in the following pages should be allowed to grow as loosely and as naturally as possible. They should never be radically pruned. On the other hand, organic gardeners should make sure that these woody plants do not just grow wild and that their branches do not grow toward the center. In order to avoid this, old or thin branches should be cut back to the ground in early spring. Similarly, branches that are growing inward and all the ones that have become intertwined with one another also ought to be removed. This will allow the younger shoots to develop and fill in various empty spaces, and the whole shrub will remain loose, healthy, and

A naturally growing loose hedge of spirea, lilacs, and laburnum.

in good shape.

The following selection also includes a few of the beautiful and well-known blooming shrubs. They can be planted together to form natural blooming hedges or else they can be featured as individual specimens and focuses of attention in a charming garden scene.

Barberries are thorny, woody plants, many varied representatives of which can be purchased in nurseries or garden centers. The natural form, *Berberis vulgaris,* makes a very good

hedge plant. These shrubs grow 3′ to 6′ tall; they are very undemanding and bear red berries, which also happen to be edible, in the fall. Barberries thrive in sun as well as in partial shade.

Rock Pears grow in the form of graceful, airy shrubs that are covered with white blossoms in the spring and with reddish-orange leaves in the fall. They flourish in dry as well as in moist soils, in direct sun and in partial shade. Height: 16′ to 26′.

Fire Thorn grows into impenetrable, thorny hedges about 6′ to 9′ tall. It

(Not Merely Ornamental) Shrubs

prefers sun and good humus, but can also thrive under less favorable conditions. The leaves remain green all year long. This shrub blooms white in the spring and produces reddish-orange berries in the fall. It is a good site for nests and a good provider of bird food.

Lilacs are charming and old-fashioned shrubs whose blossoms in May fill the whole garden with their glorious scent. Lilacs make very good, airy hedges. The shrub needs a some-

Pretty and edible: the blossoms of the elder tree.

Birds love fire thorn.

what limy soil rich in humus and direct sunlight. Nevertheless, it can also tolerate some shade. Height: 3' to 14'. In addition to the cultivars, there are very pretty natural species like *Syringa chinensis,* Chinese lilac.

Forsythia is among the first to herald the arrival of spring. This undemanding, vigorously growing shrub is covered with golden-yellow blossoms as early as March. It thrives in every kind of garden soil and can be employed in thick hedges.

Elder forms mighty shrubs that can attain a height of up to 30'. They are extremely undemanding, but thrive especially well in soils rich in humus and nutrients. The fragrant white blossoms are as edible as the black berries—if you manage to get to them before the birds do.

Cornelian Cherries are members of the large family of *Cornaceae.* The yellow blossoms begin to appear as early as February, and this makes these shrubs a good candidate for bee-and-

The red berries of the hawthorn.

butterfly gardens. The edible red fruits ripen in the fall. Cornelian cherries are undemanding and can grow even in the mountains. A moist soil containing lime is especially conducive for good growth. Height: 13' to 18'.

What is commonly called **Jasmine** is more properly described by its real name of Mock Orange (Philadelphus). These robust shrubs can easily attain a height of 4½' to 13'. They grow in every ordinary garden soil in bright sunshine as well as in partial shade. The white, saucer-shaped blossoms with their sweet and romantic fragrance appear in early summer.

European Spindle Trees are shrubs that come in many shapes. The European variety (Euonymus europaeus) grows to a height of 10' to 14', produces reddish-pink fruit in the fall, and makes very good hedges. These shrubs are undemanding: They thrive in any ordinary garden soil and even in higher altitudes.

Blackthorns grow slowly but steadily into impenetrable, thorny hedges. They are extremely tolerant, with one exception: They do not like wet soils. These shrubs are smothered with white blossoms very early in spring, and in late fall the bluish berries, which are best eaten only after the first frost, ripen gradually. Blackthorns grow between 6' and 13' tall and offer birds sanctuary and food.

Viburnum is the collective name for many shrubs that usually bear white blossom clusters. Common viburnum (Viburnum opulus "Sterile") grows about 9' tall. It is undemanding, but thrives best in direct sunlight.

Summer Lilacs should be a part of every natural garden because they lure butterflies like a magnet with their long panicles. This explains the common name for this shrub, the butterfly bush (Buddleia). Summer lilacs need a protected location with a lot of sun and a soil rich in humus. The area around the roots should be kept moist with a mulch cover. Under favorable conditions, these shrubs can reach a height of 13'.

Spiraea comes in many different species and varieties. The tall, ornamental plant (Spiraea vanhouttei) makes a very good hedge; it usually grows 4' tall and is covered with profuse white blossoms in the spring. These shrubs do not make any special demands as far as soil and location are concerned. They can thrive in the sun as well as in partial shade.

Weigelias are robust shrubs that grow in any ordinary garden soil. They are equally tolerant of sun and partial shade, and produce red or pink blossoms from June to July. Weigelias can attain a height of up to 12'.

Hawthorn is another traditional, thorny hedge shrub that offers a safe

(Not Merely Ornamental) Shrubs

nesting place for birds. It usually grows between 6' and 18' tall and is undemanding. The only things it does not like are very light soils and a high water-table level. Hawthorn grows in the sun as well as in partial shade. It produces white blossoms in the spring and edible, mealy, red berries in the fall.

Ornamental Currants flourish in any ordinary, well-drained garden soil in the sun or in partial shade. These red-blooming shrubs have a very pretty effect in the spring, but their fruit is unpalatable. These plants can grow 6' to 8' tall. Alpine currants *(Ribes alpinum)* make a very good bird sanctuary.

Good organic gardeners do not choose the plants in their gardens only for the use of birds and other small animals. The gardeners themselves want to enjoy the calm and relaxation their green oases provide. All the more reason why the shrubs that comprise a natural hedge should be so arranged that they unite the pleasant with the practical. A balmy spring evening amid fragrant lilacs brings contentment to an organic gardener after a hard day's work. This natural relaxation and the enjoyment of beautiful flowers are just as important as the serious efforts he or she expended in protecting and conserving nature.

One Last Word

If the beginning organic gardener has managed to hold out to this last page, there is a good chance that he or she has learned enough to pass the entrance exam and to put this newly acquired knowledge to practical use. Still, it is not merely a matter of success that can be demonstrated by carrots and roses. More important than anything else is the "inner conversion" of the individual. Whoever has become committed to natural gardening methods will one day look upon all plants and animals as his or her next of kin and will fully understand what Albert Schweitzer once called "reverence for life." No mouse is so insignificant that it should not be treated with the respect due a coinhabitant of this planet. Many readers will perhaps be reminded of a Bible passage: "What ye do for the least of my brothers, ye do also for me." Shouldn't this also include the earthworms, which shrivel to death under the onslaught of weed-killing herbicides? Or the lice, which, sprayed to death, drop from the trees?

Only he who fosters life will also gain life and health—for himself, his garden, and the future.

Death and destruction have not yet changed the world for the better. Not even when it is "only" a matter of insects, for on the good of the smallest depends the life of the biggest on this earth. Humility is an old-fashioned word, almost unused nowadays. Whoever does utter it runs the risk of being regarded with sympathetic and superior smiles. Organic gardeners, as well as those who want to be organic gardeners, should allow themselves at least one quiet hour to think about the meaning of this word.

Whoever gardens in keeping with the laws of nature and watches earwigs at work has no grounds to look down disparagingly upon those who march to "a different drummer." Perhaps all they need is a little longer to discover the advantages and the peace of organic gardening. More convincing than all the know-it-all kohlrabi experts are friendly neighbors and a taste or two passed over the garden fence.

If you want to be happy your whole life long . . . become an organic gardener.

Index

Index

Look for these other books in the Macmillan Gardening series

THE MACMILLAN BOOK OF NATURAL HERB GARDENING
  by Marie-Luise Kreuter

THE MACMILLAN BOOK OF ORNAMENTAL GARDENING
  by Otto Hahn

Look for these other gardening books from Macmillan

WYMAN'S GARDENING ENCYCLOPEDIA
  by Donald Wyman

THE TREASURY OF HOUSEPLANTS
  by Rob Herwig and Margot Schubert

THE MACMILLAN TREASURY OF HERBS
  by Ann Bonar